PEOPLE AND THEMES IN HOMER'S ODYSSEY

# PEOPLE AND THEMES
# IN HOMER'S ODYSSEY

## AGATHE THORNTON

## METHUEN & CO. LTD.
### 11 NEW FETTER LANE, LONDON, EC4

in association with

## UNIVERSITY OF OTAGO PRESS
### DUNEDIN

*First published in 1970*
© 1970 Agathe Thornton
SBN 416 16790 X
1. 1


*Distributed in the USA*
*by Barnes & Noble Inc.*

*Printed in New Zealand by*
*John McIndoe Limited, Dunedin*

# CONTENTS

# ABBREVIATIONS

Companion to Homer *A Companion to Homer,* ed. Wace
and Stubbings (London, 1962)

Cunliffe R. J. Cunliffe, *A Lexicon of the Homeric Dialect*
(London, 1924)

Eliade Mircea Eliade, *Shamanism: Archaic Techniques of
Ecstasy* (Paris, 1951; transl. London, 1954)

Essays on the Odyssey *Essays on the Odyssey,* ed. Charles
H. Taylor, Jr. (Indiana Univ. Press, 1963)

Finley M. I. Finley, *The World of Odysseus* (London, 1956)

Kirk G. S. Kirk, *The Songs of Homer* (Cambridge, 1962)

Merry and Riddell W. W. Merry and J. Riddell, *Homer's
Odyssey,* Books 1 to 12 (Oxford, 1886)

Monro D. B. Monro, *Homer's Odyssey,* Books 13 to 24
(Oxford, 1901)

Page D. Page, *The Homeric Odyssey* (Oxford, 1955)

R.E. Pauly-Wissowa, *Real-Encyclopädie der Classischen
Altertumswissenschaft*

Stanford W. B. Stanford, *The Odyssey of Homer* (London,
1954)

Webster T. B. L. Webster, *From Mycenae to Homer*
(London, 1958)

# PREFACE

I should like to acknowledge with warm gratitude my debt to Professor T. B. L. Webster who first suggested to me that I should collect my work on the *Odyssey* in a book, and whose interest and criticism have been invaluable to me over many years. He is, of course, not responsible for any errors that remain.

To those students of mine, who studied the *Odyssey* with me in their Honours year, I should like to give thanks for their companionship and enthusiasm and for the occasional helpful idea.

I thank the Editors of *AUMLA* for permission to use (with slight alterations) the paper on the Suitors, published in *AUMLA* 20, November 1963.

Finally, I wish to express my gratitude to my husband for his unfailing encouragement and patience, which made this work possible.

# INTRODUCTION

In getting to know a work of poetry the first thing should always be to read it as a whole and to become acquainted with it intimately as a whole. This appears to be not as obvious as it sounds. Very early a fashion must have grown up of reciting portions of the Homeric epics, either in isolation or not in the right order. For we are told[1] that Hipparchus, tyrant of Athens, 'compelled the rhapsodes at the Panathenaea to perform them according to the cues, in due order', and we know from the orator Lycurgus that this rule was still adhered to in 332 B.C. Since then this postulate, which ought to be a matter of course in relation to a great poem, has often been neglected in favour of a very different approach connected with the so-called 'Homeric Question'. At least, this is the picture presented by the history of Homeric scholarship. It is probable that many people who have not been professional scholars in the Homeric field have read and enjoyed and intimately known the Homeric epics even since the fifth century B.C.; and this is once again the case today in the English-speaking world through Rieu's and Lattimore's translations.

Homeric scholarship, on the other hand, has pursued for the most part the 'Homeric Question'. This is concerned with the history of the two epics. A historical bias is of course characteristic of the spirit of the nineteenth and the latter part of the eighteenth century. In many fields of inquiry the question of how something has come to be, that is the question of genetic or historical development, has taken precedence over the question of what something is like, how it is constructed, how it functions. Both these questions, namely what something is like, and how it came to be what it is, are perfectly legitimate with reference to any subject-matter. But the investigations pursued to answer these two questions cannot be substituted for each other. If you try to trace the history of one of the Homeric epics from internal evidence, you are not thereby describing the structure and functioning of that poem, although you may be able to suggest reasons for some strange features in it by these means. Again, if you describe the poetic stuff and shape of the poems, you do not thereby trace their history or development; and any oddities which may be remnants from that history must at least be presumed to have some function within the whole in which they appear, even if this function is no more than to add the charm of a strange antiquity. I shall call the two different approaches 'diachronic' and 'synchronic', terms introduced by De Saussure into linguistics: 'diachronic' referring to what 'goes through time', that is what develops or changes historically or genetically, and 'synchronic' referring to what is 'together in time' or 'contemporaneous'.

What has very largely happened in Homeric criticism is this, that synchronic investigation, that is the investigation of the poems as they stand, has been given very short shrift, or—and this is worse—it has been pursued with inadequate criteria. The consequence has been the discovery of a famous series of 'inconsistencies' or 'anomalies' which have then been made starting-points for the most extravagant speculations about the diachronic genesis of the two poems.

There are two criteria which are often applied uncritically and which are quite pernicious in their effect on Homeric criticism. The first is what we from our twentieth century point of view call 'logical'; the second is what we call 'first-rate poetry', or again 'second-rate'. The first type of judgement is rationalistic, the second aesthetic. Both are in the form in which they usually appear firmly anchored in modern forms of thought, and quite the wrong sort to use in relation to Homeric epic: in fact they are 'anachronistic'. What is needed instead of an unbridled 'historicism' is real historical sense, namely the realization that in the Homeric world not only houses, weapons, and customs were very different from our own, but also forms of thought, judgements on conduct, beauty, excellence, social institutions and so on. Much has been done on this kind of line: Jaeger's *Paideia,* Finley's *World of Odysseus* are examples. Books such as these, while they have their own intrinsic interest, are in relation to the synchronic investigation of the poems tools only, but important tools. For they describe no more than the presuppositions which underlie the poet's work. Partly he is not conscious of them, but works in terms of them as a matter of course. Partly he uses them as material to be moulded into poetry. It is the interpreter's or literary critic's task to find out how he has used them.

The relationship between synchronic and diachronic investigation in Homeric criticism is complicated by the fact that the critics are, for the most part, divided into two camps: the Analysts and the Unitarians. The Analysts, starting from inconsistencies and other difficulties, construct a hypothesis concerning the genesis of this difficulty and of the parts of the epic in which it occurs, the underlying assumption being that of a number of authors, 'multiple authorship', as it is called. The work of Analysts is often brief and uncritical in the way described above as far as synchronic investigation is concerned, and often highly ingenious in the construction of diachronic theories. The Unitarians work synchronically when they try to show by interpretation of the work as it stands that those 'inconsistencies' or other difficulties do not in fact exist. Hereby they deny that the particular passage under discussion offers any foothold for diachronic investigation. This does not mean of course that a Unitarian today necessarily denies the possibility of diachronic work. Both archaeology and linguistics are now supplying criteria which can be used with some confidence, if with caution, in diachronic investigation.

But, quite apart from criteria of this external sort, the nature of the Homeric Question has been changed fundamentally by Milman Parry's and A. B. Lord's conclusive demonstration that the Homeric epics were composed in the tradition of oral poetry, whether they were in fact written down by the poet or dictated by him, or handed down orally by the 'Sons of Homer'. If the Homeric epics are oral poetry, the old

alternative between single authorship and multiple authorship has disappeared. To the diachronic point of view,
multiple authorship is certain: for four to five centuries at least
each bard standing in the tradition of oral epic poetry would
take over from his teachers and colleagues anything that they
offered in their songs and use it according to his own taste and
ability. To the synchronic point of view, each bard, at any one
performance, composed anew in his singing what had been
handed down to him. Therefore single and multiple authorship are no longer an either-or, but they are both true and—
one must add emphatically—inextricably wrought into each
other. We may sometimes feel that we can see the hand of
the last great poet, Homer himself, but we can never be sure.
Let us consider the kind of thing that must happen in oral
traditional poetry.

Let us take a young singer producing his song at a specific
occasion before a particular audience as the starting-point for
our thinking. A year later he may sing a song on the same
subject a little more elaborated in part. Twenty or thirty
years later his song on this subject may be highly complex
and dramatic, while in parts it may be brief to the point of
being unintelligible, because he has lost interest in these particular parts. Suppose we had the written text of the three
versions without name of author, could we decide how many
authors there were? It is very doubtful. Supposing again that
this man's pupil has a good ear and memory, but little spontaneous imagination and initiative, might not the pupil's
versions, particularly his earlier ones, be closer to his master's
late versions than the master's late versions to those of his
youth? We might be tempted to assign the early version of a
great singer to one person and his later version and that of his
follower to another. The conclusion from all this must be I
think that to determine conclusively earlier forms of our epics
is beyond our reach. This conclusion holds for a poem that
is composed within or directly derived from a tradition of oral
poetry, and consequently holds for the *Iliad* and the *Odyssey,*
the traditional oral character of which has been demonstrated
by Parry and Lord.

But there is still the possibility that our poems may contain

799-700 BC = 8th cent

minor alterations or additions stemming from a time later than the probable date of composition, which is the end of the eighth century B.C. On the other hand, it can no longer be assumed that any considerable portion of a book or a whole book, like Book 24 in the *Odyssey* or Book 10 in the *Iliad,* was not part of the poet's plan for his poem, since that plan seems to imply from the beginning the present number of books. For J. A. Davison[2] has shown for the *Iliad* that while single books vary considerably in length (Book 5: 909 lines, Book 19: 424 lines), groups of four books vary proportionately much less, the lowest number of lines being 2304 for Books 17 to 20 and the highest being 2927 for Books 13 to 16, one sixth of all the lines of the *Iliad* (15683) being 2614. On the basis of experimentation, Davison assumes that a 'reasonable speed for the public recitation of Greek hexameters to a continuing audience is about eleven lines a minute'. The average recitation of a 4 book group from the *Iliad* would take just under four hours. Davison suggests that the epic would be recited over three days, with two sessions each day, by a team of four reciters, each reciting one book in each session. However that may be, corresponding numerical relations obtain in the *Odyssey*. The figures of the six groups are

| Books | | | |
|---|---|---|---|
| | 1 to | 4 | 2222 |
| | 5 to | 8 | 1757 |
| | 9 to | 12 | 2233 |
| | 13 to | 16 | 2011 |
| | 17 to | 20 | 2032 |
| | 21 to | 24 | 1855 |

The average number of lines is 2019, and would take just over three hours to recite. Davison notes the following: 'Odysseus breaks off his narrative in *Od.* 11.330 after the equivalent of 1,470 hexameters; being adjured to go on, he then continues for a further 714 lines (or at about eleven lines to the minute, approximately 3h. 20m. actual narration, with a short break for general conversation just after two-thirds of the whole story)'.[3] This means that the narrative of the wanderings of Odysseus himself, which fills the best part of four books, takes about a quarter of an hour longer than the average of the six groups of four books each. This seems to make it certain, so far as number of lines and time go, that the division into groups of four books is right in relation to a bard's or reciter's performance. Davison is hesitant about attributing too much importance to such purely numerical findings, but if an analysis of the content of the epic leads to the same grouping, then the matter becomes incontrovertible. Such an analysis will be attempted at the end of this book, when I hope that a number of crippling difficulties in interpretation will have been removed.

The Studies which form the body of this book are, for the most part, synchronic. Only the second part of chapter II on the origins of the wanderings of Odysseus is strictly diachronic. In all the others attention is concentrated on the poet's work as it comes to meet us in the texts which we have.

Two lines of interpretation in particular have been pursued, determined both of them by the sort of poetry that the Homeric epics are. The first is concerned with the way in which certain themes are used in the composition of the poem; the second arises from the primarily dramatic quality of the *Odyssey*.

A. B. Lord[4] says that a Yugoslav singer told him 'that when he learned a new song he made no attempt at word-for-word memorization but learned only the "plan" of the song, which he explained as "the arrangement of the events". This plan he then proceeded to fill in with the themes which he already knew.' In Part I a number of themes that occur in the *Odyssey* are described. The themes of 'omens', 'guest-friendship' and perhaps also 'testing' are both social institutions and bardic themes. The wanderings and returns of the Achaeans and the wanderings of Odysseus are certainly traditional themes of the singers. Where necessary the theme is analysed in detail in order to show the traditional pattern of its sequence. In all five chapters the manner of poetic presentation is investigated. Some themes run through the whole epic illuminating the action at key-points, others are 'ornamented', as the Yugoslav singers would say,[5] with great variety. Most of them are also important for the presentation of the characters in Part II. In the description of the characters, I have aimed rather at removing obstacles to understanding and at indicating specific aspects than at completeness. This is particularly true of the chapters on Telemachus and Odysseus. The manner of interpretation is largely determined by the highly dramatic character of the *Odyssey*. Plato says about epic in general that it stands midway between tragedy and comedy on the one hand, and the poet himself telling a story, as for instance in dithyrambs, on the other.[6] In tragedy and comedy the actions and utterances of people are 'imitated' directly; in dithyrambs they are narrated by the poet. Epic partakes of both. Aristotle, speaking specifically about Homer, praises him in contrast to other epic poets for commenting little himself, but narrating instead how his characters act and speak.[7] This means that the Homeric epics have to be interpreted to a considerable extent, like plays. Only occasionally does the poet show his mind and intention directly. Mostly, the audience or reader has to infer what is intended from the actions and speeches of the characters in their relations to each other; and—I must add emphatically—not only in one scene at a time, but always in relation to all that precedes the scene under discussion. This is obvious of course in drama; it also applies to Homer's *Odyssey*.

Polemic is largely kept out of the text, and relegated to the notes. But much that is discussed owes its original stimulus to 'anomalies' pointed out by scholars of the 'analytical' school.

# PART I

# THEMES AND COMPOSITION IN THE ODYSSEY

## CHAPTER I

# THE HOMECOMINGS OF THE ACHAEANS

### *Their Function in the Poem*

The homecomings of the Achaeans after the fall of Troy offered a wealth of material for the epic singer. He might sing of the return of Agamemnon, of Menelaus, of Nestor, of Diomedes, of Odysseus and others. The poet of our *Odyssey* chose to sing the homecoming of Odysseus. But he did not therefore exclude all the others; he worked a number of them into the composition of his poem with various purposes in view. We will consider first the functions fulfilled by these Achaean return-stories; and secondly the manner in which they are told.

The most prominent of the Achaean homecomings throughout the *Odyssey* is that of Agamemnon, which is set into relation to each one of the main actors in the poem: to the Suitors, Telemachus, Odysseus and Penelope.

In his opening speech at the beginning of the divine assembly Zeus speaks pensively of Aegisthus who was killed by Orestes, son of Agamemnon: 'Alas, how mortals blame the gods! For they say that evils come from us. But they themselves also by their own outrageous deeds suffer beyond their destiny, as now Aegisthus has married beyond his destiny the wedded wife of Agamemnon, and killed him himself when he came home, although he knew the steep destruction (that threatened him). For we told him beforehand, sending Hermes, the sharp-sighted Argus-killer, not to kill him, nor to marry his wife: "For vengeance will come for Agamemnon from Orestes, when he has reached manhood and longs for his native land". Thus spoke Hermes. But he did not persuade the mind of Aegisthus, however kindly he was disposed; and now Aegisthus has paid the penalty for it all'.[1]

Noble Aegisthus married the absent king's wife, Clytemnestra, seized his kingship, and killed King Agamemnon himself on his return. Agamemnon's son, Orestes, when grown to manhood, came home and killed Aegisthus to avenge his father. The nobles of Ithaca woo the absent king's wife, Penelope. They have every intention of killing Odysseus if he should come home and want to drive them out of his house.[2] Antinous and Eurymachus have in mind to usurp the kingship, as we shall see, and kill Telemachus. When Telemachus has come to be a man, and Odysseus has returned in disguise, the two kill the Suitors in revenge for their evil deeds. The parallelism is unmistakable and has often been pointed out.[3]

Zeus' speech makes a brilliant beginning, precisely because its relevance is not immediately evident. The person of whom Zeus thinks first and foremost is Aegisthus, his criminal actions in spite of forewarnings, and his punishment by death at the hands of Orestes. Why does Homer introduce the homecoming of Agamemnon in this oblique way? Why is Agamemnon himself, counterpart of Odysseus, not in the centre of the story of his return? There are two reasons for this. First, in Books 1 and 2, the outrageous actions and intentions of the Suitors are represented, and they are forewarned by the words of Telemachus, by omen and prophecy, just as Aegisthus was forewarned.[4] Zeus' speech leads therefore directly into the action at Ithaca. Secondly, by placing the crimes of Aegisthus and their punishment at the beginning, Homer indicates the moral and religious theme which pervades his *Odyssey*: that outrageous actions are punished by the decree of Zeus. In fact, Zeus' speech is 'programmatic', as E. R. Dodds puts it.[5]

This theme is not only worked out in the action of the epic when the Suitors are punished by death, but it is constantly kept to the fore in the characterization of the Suitors. The key words are 'insolence' (*hybris*) and 'violence' (*bie*).

Athene disguised as Mentes, watching the Suitors, says that they 'seem to feast in the house with excessive wantonness', perpetrating 'much that is disgraceful'.[6] When Telemachus addresses the Suitors he calls them 'Suitors of my mother, men of insolence and violence'.[7] This characterization even crystallizes into formulae.[8] When Antinous, the leading prince among the Suitors, hurls a stool at the beggar Odysseus, even his own associates are taken aback and wonder whether the beggar might be a god in disguise. For 'in the likeness of strangers from afar, the gods in various forms wander through the cities watching the wantonness and the "good and orderly life of men" '.[9] The matter is stated by Odysseus himself when, in reply to Eurymachus' entreaty, he refuses to spare the Suitors; not for any gifts whatever would he stop his hand from slaying 'until the Suitors had paid the penalty for all their transgression';[10] and Eurycleia, exulting over the bodies of the Suitors, is checked by Odysseus, who realizes that the Suitors' death is brought about by the gods and their own evil deeds, and that they owe their shameful end to their own 'wilful folly'.[11] Further bloodshed is prevented by Zeus, who causes the kinsfolk of the dead Suitors to 'forget the killing of their sons and brothers'.[12] This presents a first inkling of a transition from the endlessly destructive justice of kin blood-vengeance to a more humane justice of the gods, as Hommel has shown, who connects this with the mercy of Athene at the end of Aeschylus' *Eumenides*.[13]

Zeus' speech about Aegisthus states then the religious and ethical theme of divine justice worked out in the *Odyssey* in the actions and fate of the Suitors.

The tale of Agamemnon's homecoming ends in young Orestes slaying Aegisthus, the murderer of his father. Our poet has used this part of the story in relation to Telemachus: Orestes, the famous avenger of his father, is set as a glorious example before Telemachus by Athene and by Nestor in order to rouse him to action.[14] This is well known, and needs no further explanation.

Agamemnon himself is brought into relation with Odysseus and indirectly with Penelope. In the Underworld the two heroes meet. Agamemnon describes his death at the hand of Aegisthus and Clytemnestra's betrayal; and then, speaking out of his own experience, warns Odysseus not to trust Penelope, however sensible she is, and not to return to his place openly but in secret.[15]

When Athene and Odysseus meet again for the first time after Odysseus' arrival on Ithaca, Athene tells Odysseus about the Suitors in the palace, and he replies that he would have perished in the same evil fashion as Agamemnon, had the goddess not told him everything.[16] The outcome is of course that Athene turns Odysseus into an old beggar so that he may be unrecognizable and return home in concealment as Agamemnon had suggested.[17]

Finally the lots of Agamemnon, Achilles, the Suitors and indirectly Odysseus are brought together in the second Underworld scene at the beginning of the last book of the epic. This scene needs detailed interpretation as it has not been understood.

The second Underworld scene is a carefully constructed whole. It is introduced by Hermes guiding the spirits of the dead Suitors from the palace at Ithaca down to the asphodel fields of the dead. Hermes is in this scene a guide of souls. He is also a god of sleep and waking, because he is described as 'charming the eyes of men with his staff' and waking them from sleep.[18] He is a god of sleep among the Phaeacians who make to him the last libation in the day when they are on the point of going to bed.[19] Sleep and Death are brothers in the *Iliad*;[20] and they together carry the body of slain Sarpedon to Lycia at Zeus' command, being called 'swift guides' or 'conductors'.[21] Here it is of course the body, and not the spirit, that is carried off after death; and Sarpedon, a son of Zeus, is a special case. But what is plain is the close conjunction of function between death and sleep in Homeric thought. Hermes as god of sleep and guide of the dead is firmly embedded in this context. While most of the time the spirits of the dead leave their bodies and go to Hades without a guide, apart from Hermes in our passage, the *Keres,* death goddesses or daemons, are twice said to 'carry' them off.[22] But there are specific reasons for Hermes to be represented as guide of the Suitors' souls at the beginning of the last book of the *Odyssey*.

This passage is closely linked with the end of the previous book, being both parallel and contrasted. There Athene leads Odysseus, Telemachus, Philoetius and Eumaeus out of the town with the first light already on the earth, but she hides them in night. While the Suitors are led, squeaking like bats that flit about in the inner recesses of a big cave, over a mouldy path at last to where 'live the souls, images of those who have become tired', Odysseus and his companions emerge, after the Underworld scene, at the rich well-cultivated farm of Laertes, ready for action.[23] Here, at the end of the epos, Athene and Hermes work in concert, though on parallel lines, as they did at the beginning. In Book 1 Athene suggests that, while Hermes should go to Calypso and tell her to release Odysseus, she herself will go to Ithaca and rouse Telemachus.[24] She does so, and Hermes goes to Calypso in Book 5. The collaboration of Athene and Hermes seems in fact to be traditional: Heracles was accompanied by Hermes and Athene when he fetched Cerberus from the Underworld.[25]

Furthermore, this journey of the Suitors' spirits into Hades is prepared for earlier.[26] In his uncanny vision of the doomed Suitors Theoclymenus says: 'The forehall is full of ghosts, and the courtyard is full of them, hastening towards the Underworld down below the darkness.'[27] When the battle in the palace is finished, the bodies of the slain Suitors lie in a heap, like a pile of fish cast on to the beach:[28] nothing is said about their spirits going to Hades. Later their bodies are shifted from the hall to the porch outside and stacked leaning against each other:[29] again nothing about their spirits. Then, Hermes calls them out and sets them moving with his staff.[30] The god's command is needed to initiate the spirits' departure, since a whole book has passed by since the Suitors' death.

Having arrived on the field of asphodel, Hermes and the spirits of the Suitors 'found' Achilles accompanied by Patroclus, Antilochus and Ajax.[31] These four heroes are mentioned together by Nestor as having died before Troy; and in the first Underworld scene Achilles is described as being accompanied by the other three in almost identical lines.[32] 'And close came the spirit of Agamemnon, son of Atreus', accompanied by all those who died with him in the house of

Aegisthus. After a short speech by Achilles, Agamemnon describes to Achilles in great detail the glory and the honours with which he was buried, concluding with a reference to his own wretched death. 'Thus they spoke to each other in such a way; and close to them came the Guide of souls, Killer of Argus, leading down the spirits of the Suitors vanquished by Odysseus.'[33] The sequence of events is strange here. If it is taken to be chronological, it does not make sense, because Hermes leading the Suitors seems to arrive among the spirits twice over.[34] The clue to the apparent confusion lies in the use of the word 'they found' the spirit of Achilles.[35] Cunliffe[36] gives as one shade of meaning of this verb 'to find or come upon in a specified place or condition or doing something specified'. When in the second book of the *Iliad* everyone was rushing to the ships after Agamemnon's speech, Athene 'then found Odysseus, like unto Zeus in intelligence, standing; and he did not touch the black ship with the good rowing benches since grief filled his heart and spirit. Standing close by him owl-eyed Athene spoke to him.'[37] Here the verb 'found' is followed by over two lines describing Odysseus' attitude and feelings, and then by Athene approaching him and speaking to him. The form of presentation is the same when Iris 'finds' Helen, whose weaving and tragic role is described before Iris approaches her,[38] and again when the Ambassadors 'find' Achilles who is described in over five lines as singing to his lyre and having Patroclus sitting beside him, before they step forward, and stand in front of him.[39] The common shape of such a scene is then: (1) finding a person, (2) description of the person's state, etc., (3) approaching that person and talking. In the case of Nestor, who was 'found' by Agamemnon arranging and exhorting his troops, the second part, that is the description, is seventeen lines long and includes a speech to his men of seven lines.[40]

In the *Odyssey* Telemachus and Pisistratus 'found' Menelaus giving a wedding-feast for a son and daughter of his to his fellow townsmen.[41] Particulars about the two marriages are given, and about the son born from a slave woman, since Helen had not borne another child after Hermione. After this expansion we return to the wedding-feast which is accompanied by a bard's song and the swift circling of two acrobats. Then at last Telemachus and his friend stand at the porch, and contact is made through Eteoneus seeing them. Here the description of Menelaus giving a feast and all the explanation that is added spans over sixteen lines, the explanations in part referring to the past.[42] Finally in Book 5 Calypso found Odysseus 'sitting on the beach, and never did his eyes become dry of tears'.[43] Through the word 'never' the description is immediately widened to comprise the past as well as the present; and the verbs 'he used to spend the night' and 'he used to look out' (to sea) convey the same. After seven lines of such a description of what he had been doing for a long time, Calypso stands close to him and addresses him.[44]

Our passage in Book 24 appears to be shaped on this pattern. Firstly, Hermes and the Suitors 'found' the spirit of Achilles and his friends.[45] Thirdly, Hermes leading the Suitors 'came close to them.'[46] What is in between must be the description of the state in which Hermes finds Achilles.[47] It consists actually of Agamemnon approaching Achilles, who greets him, and a long speech of Agamemnon which exalts Achilles through the detailed description of his funeral before Troy: he is the most glorious of the heroes that have died in the war. So far as chronological time is concerned this meeting between Agamemnon and Achilles would precede Hermes' arrival; the movement into the past between line 15 and line 19 which we who usually think in chronological time must postulate is not noticed by the poet: what matters is that Achilles stands glorified, though a dead spirit, by Agamemnon when Hermes and the dead Suitor Amphimedon come to meet him.

There is another chronological difficulty in connection with this conversation between Achilles and Agamemnon. The actual sequence of events is this: Achilles falls before Troy; Troy is conquered; Agamemnon on his return home is murdered; Odysseus speaks to Agamemnon and Achilles in the Underworld in Book 11; Odysseus on his return home kills the Suitors whose spirits arrive in the Underworld in Book 24.

In our passage Agamemnon and Achilles converse, as if Agamemnon had just arrived from the world of the living.

Chronologically speaking, this conversation should take place before the events in Book 11. We must ask ourselves whether the poet could have had a particular reason for placing this conversation where it is, a reason strong enough to make the awkwardness of sequence of no account.[48]

In order to understand the function of the conversation between Achilles and Agamemnon, it must be considered in relation to the subsequent conversation between Agamemnon and the Suitor Amphimedon.[49]

The connectedness of the two dialogues is formally indicated in two ways. In each part Agamemnon praises a hero as blessed at the beginning of a speech: Achilles first, 'blessed son of Peleus', in line 36, and then the absent Odysseus, 'blessed son of Laertes', in line 192. Each part is rounded off by the line: 'Thus they spoke such things to each other', in the second part one further line being added: 'the twain standing in the house of Hades below the covering of the earth'.[50] 'The twain' refers to Agamemnon and Amphimedon, who have been talking together, Achilles being forgotten. This dual form corresponds to the duals in line 101, 'the twain full of amazement then went straight towards him when they saw him'. These duals refer to Achilles and Agamemnon, the pair of speakers in the first part. There are then two clearly marked parts with a pair of speakers in each.

In each part the ghost of a dead hero receives someone who approaches him and gives him news about events that have happened on earth since his death. Thus Achilles hears of his funeral from Agamemnon; and Agamemnon hears of the Suitors' fate at the hands of Penelope and Odysseus. In each part the receiving ghost makes a brief speech (11 and 14 lines), and the approaching ghost a long speech (62 and 70/69 lines), Agamemnon's brief reply (11 lines) rounding off the scene.

The content of the two long speeches is the description of Achilles' splendid funeral and the account of the death of the Suitors still lying unburied. The one speaks of the glory of dead Achilles, the other of the winning of life and fame by Odysseus through causing the death of his enemies. In the two long speeches Achilles and Odysseus are set in contrast.

This theme does not appear here for the first time. When Telemachus asks Nestor to tell him of his father's death[51]— he does not believe that he might be alive—Nestor tells him that Ajax is dead, and Achilles, and Patroclus, and his son Antilochus, the same heroes that as spirits surround Achilles in Book 24. But he knows nothing about Odysseus. The death of Achilles and the question of whether Odysseus is dead or alive appear side by side. In Book 8 the theme of Demodocus' first song[52] is the 'Quarrel of Odysseus and Achilles, son of Peleus', a famous song, in which in all probability Achilles spoke on behalf of 'might' and Odysseus on behalf of 'guile', the third song being praise of the Wooden Horse which means the victory of Odysseus' guile. Once again Achilles and Odysseus are brought together by the poet: in the Underworld, face to face, Achilles a ghost, but Odysseus a live man. Achilles has with him the same friends who died with him according to Nestor. Odysseus explains his coming to the Underworld, and then he praises Achilles: 'In comparison with you, Achilles, no man in the past has ever been very blessed nor will be in future. For formerly when you were alive we Argives honoured you like unto the gods, and now again you rule mightily among the dead, being here. Therefore, though dead, do not grieve, Achilles!'[53] Achilles' answer is well-known, that he would rather be the servant of a poor man on the earth than ruler of all the dead below the earth. It is this scene that Homer wants his audience to recall when he once again in Book 24 leads us into the Underworld. There Achilles makes no reply when Agamemnon praises him as blessed and describes the marvellous glory of his funeral. But we know that to Achilles sheer life is what he values most, and the description of the great funeral becomes suffused with sadness. In contrast to Achilles, Odysseus does not appear in the Underworld because he is alive, and further he is victorious over his enemies, because he has practised guile more than might. The long train of dead Suitors testifies to his glory.

Between Achilles and Odysseus stands Agamemnon. He calls them both blessed: the one has fame, but is dead; the other is alive, and has fame; but he himself has fought the Trojan War to the end, it is true, but there is no joy in that.[54]

He had neither a glorious funeral before Troy, like Achilles; nor is he alive and returned to power at home, like Odysseus. Therefore he concludes by praising Odysseus on account of the good sense and faithfulness of Penelope, so utterly different from Clytemnestra who killed her husband, Agamemnon.

It is at this point and in Book 11 that the story of Agamemnon's fateful return is connected also with Penelope. In Book 11 Agamemnon warns Odysseus not, or at least not wholly, to trust Penelope even though he acknowledges the excellence of her mind and character.[55] But at the end of the Underworld scene in Book 24 Agamemnon praises Penelope without reserve for her 'great virtue' in contrast to the evil deeds of his own wife, Clytemnestra.[56]

To sum up, the meaning of the Underworld scene in Book 24 is an assessment of the fates and achievements of Agamemnon, Achilles and Odysseus, an assessment by which Odysseus emerges as the greatest of them all, and that, according to Agamemnon, thanks to Penelope. Here the story of Agamemnon's return together with the death of Achilles before Troy is the sombre background for the glory of Odysseus and Penelope.

The homecomings of Nestor and Menelaus are more restricted both in scope and relevance. Told in Books 3 and 4 they give a picture of the wider world of Odysseus, beyond the bounds of Ithaca itself; and so they form a general backdrop to Odysseus' own wanderings which begin with Book 5.[57] The function of the homecoming of Menelaus is also more specific. For the climax of his tale is the prophecy of Proteus about Odysseus being a prisoner of Calypso, which leads of course directly to Book 5, the book describing Odysseus on Ogygia with Calypso. Furthermore, Menelaus in his home with Helen and looking forward to eternal life in Elysium is, as W. S. Anderson has shown, set in contrast by the poet to Odysseus staying with Calypso, but setting forth on his journey to Ithaca.[58]

## Their Narrative Structure

In Book 1 the bard sings 'the grievous homecoming of the Achaeans from Troy which Pallas Athene inflicted on them'.[59]

This grievous homecoming is described by Nestor in Book 3, by Menelaus in Book 4, and by Agamemnon in Book 11.[60]

In reply to Telemachus' question Nestor tells his tale. When after nine years of war the Achaeans embarked in their ships, 'then Zeus planned in his heart a grievous homecoming for the Argives, since they were not all sensible or just. Therefore many of them fulfilled an evil fate arising from the deathly anger of the bright-eyed daughter of a mighty father who caused strife between the two sons of Atreus'.[61] Why Athene was angry we are not told. The strife arose in a disorderly drunken assembly held at night: Agamemnon wanted to stay until he had reconciled Athene by sacrifices, but Menelaus wanted to leave. Half of the Achaeans stayed with Agamemnon, the other half, among them Nestor, sailed with Menelaus to Tenedos. Here another quarrel arose, and Odysseus separated off, favouring Agamemnon. Then Nestor fled, recognizing the wrath of the gods, and with him Diomedes. At Lesbus they were overtaken by Menelaus; and they sailed together across the open Aegaean to Geraistus on Euboia. From there Diomedes went to Argus, and Nestor to Pylus with a good wind.

This is the homecoming of Nestor and Diomedes which Nestor concludes with the words: 'Thus I arrived, dear child, without any news, and as far as my own experience goes I know nothing about who of the Achaeans were saved and who perished.'[62] Let us notice here that we have left Agamemnon at Troy, Odysseus at Tenedus, and Menelaus at Geraistus in Euboia.

Nestor then proceeds to tell Telemachus what he has ascertained by hearsay since he returned home. Neoptolemus, Philoctetes, and Idomeneus returned safely; but Agamemnon was killed by Aegisthus, and avenged by Orestes, a great example for Telemachus! From this the conversation turns to the state of affairs in Ithaca and back to Agamemnon and Aegisthus, until Telemachus asks Nestor how Agamemnon died, and where Menelaus was at the time, probably wandering about and not in Argus. Nestor agrees at once: if Menelaus had returned home while Aegisthus was alive, Menelaus would have been killed without burial.[63] 'For Aegisthus had contrived a great work.'[64] While the Achaeans sat before Troy he had won Clytemnestra for himself against her better judgement, and had left the bard who was to protect her to die on an empty island. Then he made many sacrifices to the gods, having achieved what he never hoped to achieve. The question of Telemachus about Agamemnon's death is not answered here. But we are told part of the prehistory of that death.

Next Nestor in his tale sets out from Troy once more to go with Menelaus, his close friend. But at sacred Sunium Apollo killed Menelaus' helmsman, so that he was delayed by the burial of his comrade and deprived of an excellent helmsman who might have saved him much trouble. For when he too came to the cape of Maleia[65] Zeus sent a storm which split up his fleet, driving part of it towards Crete where the ships foundered, but the men were saved; the remaining five ships with Menelaus he drove to Egypt where Menelaus gathered much treasure. In the meantime Aegisthus had ruled at Mycenae for seven years after killing Agamemnon and was killed in the eighth by Orestes. On the very day when Orestes gave to the Argives a funeral feast in honour of Clytemnestra and Aegisthus, Menelaus arrived home with all his treasure. Nestor accordingly advises Telemachus to go and see Menelaus who would probably have further news.

What is the relationship between the two tales of Nestor? In the first tale, Nestor sets out from Troy with half the Achaeans. At Tenedus Odysseus departs after a quarrel; at Lesbus Menelaus catches up with Nestor and Diomedes who have fled in haste. They sail together to Euboia. Nestor and Diomedes go home. In the second tale Nestor leaves Troy with Menelaus. At Sunium Menelaus is detained by the death of his helmsman and then is driven to Egypt from where he returns home. Each time a complete homecoming is told, that is a journey from Troy to the homeland. But the two tales are clearly distinguished in that the first tale is told by an eyewitness, Nestor himself, the second from hearsay. The first also represents in some detail the drunken, quarrelsome assembly which caused the scattered return of the Achaeans. The first tale, then, is the homecoming of Nestor with his companion Diomedes, told by Nestor himself. The second tale comprises the prehistory of Agamemnon's death, told from hearsay, which makes us expect a description of Agamemnon's death at some time or other in the poem, and the homecoming of Menelaus, also by hearsay, at least from Sunium on. It is noteworthy that in the telling of this homecoming no reference is made back to the first tale: no mention of the quarrel or Odysseus or Diomedes or the details of the journey between Troy and Euboia. But Menelaus and Nestor are taken from Troy straight to Sunium. The second tale is in fact a supplement to or explanation of the first tale without this being made in any way explicit; it is also a continuation since —implicitly at least—Menelaus had been left at Geraistus in Euboia. This method of piecemeal, supplementary narration is characteristically Homeric, as Schadewaldt has pointed out.[66] But it is here complicated by the difficulty of telling parallel sequences of events. This sort of thing is managed without trouble where the parallel events are told briefly, as in Book 3 where the contemporaneity of Aegisthus' deeds and Menelaus' wanderings is expressed by *tophra*,[67] but the much more extensive contemporaneous sequences of the homecomings of Nestor (and Diomedes) and of Menelaus (at the beginning with Nestor) are not told as contemporaneous but as two separate sequences without relation to each other.

In Book 4 Menelaus tells about his own homecoming, again in two speeches.

Telemachus, full of admiration for Menelaus' wealth, whispers to Pisistratus, and Menelaus overhears his words. He explains how after much suffering and much wandering he brought his treasures home in the eighth year.[68] Expanding on his wanderings, he says that he went to Cyprus, Phoenicia and Egypt, to the Ethiopians, Sidonians, Erembi, and to Libya about which he gives some detail. But during his absence his brother was killed by some man through his wife's deceitfulness. And now Menelaus is sad, mourning those who died before Troy and grieving for Odysseus who is lost in the unknown. Here we have in fact a further expansion on the homecoming of Menelaus, but it is not told as part of a homecoming. It is told with strict relevance to the situation as an explanation for his great wealth.

The next day Menelaus asks Telemachus what he has come for, and Telemachus asks him for news of his father. Then Menelaus tells him all 'that the unerring man of the sea told him'.[69] It is unnecessary to retell the story of how Proteus, the ancient many-formed herd of seals, was caught: Menelaus relates what he has lived through himself, and the detail is vivid down to the smells. Enfolded within the Proteus story are the homecomings. For Menelaus asks him whether all the Achaeans whom he and Nestor left behind at Troy had come home safely in their ships. Proteus relates how Ajax, son of Oileus, was drowned by Poseidon for his boastfulness off the Euboian rocks of Gyrae. Then he tells of Agamemnon's home-coming in some detail. A storm carried Agamemnon to the part of the land where Aegisthus lived, but the gods sent him a wind which safely carried him further homewards; and he stepped gladly ashore and kissed his native land. The fact that Agamemnon is almost forced to land by the very house of Aegisthus, but gets safely away, is pointless to us: it indi-cates a portion of Agamemnon's homecoming which we do not know. Perhaps in this part Agamemnon's falling into the hands of Aegisthus was brought close, but dramatically retarded again. What happened after that is related in detail: the guard who waited a year for the payment of two talents of gold, the ambush of twenty men, the preparation for a banquet, Aegisthus' fetching Agamemnon and killing him at the dinner table, like an ox at the crib, and the death of all the followers of both Agamemnon and Aegisthus. Whether Menelaus will find Aegisthus alive or already killed by Orestes and being buried, is left open. We know the answer already from Nestor's story.[70] Having recovered from his first grief, Menelaus asks about Odysseus and hears about Calypso keeping him a prisoner. Finally Menelaus returns to the river Egypt and makes sacrifices, as Proteus told him to do, and then returns home to his own country.

Ostensibly, Proteus' story is told for the sake of the infor-mation which it contains about Odysseus. It is also a rich expansion on Menelaus' time in Egypt already mentioned by Nestor[71] and by Menelaus himself in his earlier speech.[72] It contains also a grievous homecoming of Ajax, son of Oileus;

and furthermore what we have been led to expect: the story of Agamemnon's return and death in some detail. Here the story begun by Nestor of how Aegisthus beguiled and won Clytemnestra finds its due completion in the account of Proteus. Let us notice however that the voyage of Nestor is told by Nestor himself, the story of Proteus by Menelaus, and the story of Agamemnon is so far told by Nestor and Menelaus who heard it from others.

In the book of the Underworld, through the mouth of Odysseus, Agamemnon himself describes his death.[73] How Aegisthus together with Clytemnestra invited him to his house and killed him at the dinner table, like an ox at the crib—the simile is repeated from Proteus' description[74]—how his friends lay dead, like pigs slaughtered for a banquet in a rich man's house, how pitifully the dead lay, not on the battlefield, but among mixing bowls and tables laden with food: 'and the whole floor was running with blood'.[75] Both the picture of the slain in the midst of a banquet and the last half line point forward to the death of the Suitors.[76] The death of Cassandra at Clytemnestra's hands, how Agamemnon died at last, and how Clytemnestra kept away from him are further new details. Clytemnestra was not mentioned in Proteus' account. The most terrible part of Agamemnon's death is told by himself, namely the part that Clytemnestra played in it.[77]

From the point of view of content the Agamemnon passage in Book 11 is an expansion on Proteus' tale. What gives it new intensity and power is the fact that it is told by the murdered man himself, as Nestor told of his own voyage, and Menelaus told of his meeting with Proteus himself.

It is great praise for a poet to be told, as Odysseus tells Demodocus, that he sings the fate of the Achaeans like one who was present himself or heard it from an eye-witness.[78] In the tales of the Achaeans' homecomings Homer has aimed at this very immediacy of presentation by putting the most detailed and intense description of events into the mouths of those who experienced them themselves.[79]

# CHAPTER II

# THE WANDERINGS OF ODYSSEUS

## *Calypso and Phaeacia*

Of all the adventures of Odysseus, which number over a dozen, only two are described directly and in full detail by the poet himself. These two are Odysseus' stay at or rather departure from Ogygia, island of Calypso, and his stay with the Phaeacians. All the other adventures are told by Odysseus to a Phaeacian audience so that they are, as it were, encapsulated within his stay in Phaeacia. Why has Homer selected the two episodes of Calypso and Phaeacia for direct, full description?

The two episodes are shaped as a contrast. On Calypso's island Odysseus spends his days sitting on the shore weeping, breaking his heart with tears, groans and sorrow, looking out to sea.[1] Calypso, the 'Concealer', has kept him there for seven years,[2] and he has had no means of escape. Even when Zeus sends Hermes to Calypso to demand Odysseus' departure, he stipulates that his journey from her island is to be undertaken 'without safe-conduct of gods or mortal men', 'but on a much-roped boat, suffering pains he shall on the twentieth day arrive at Scheria with its fine clods of earth, the land of the Phaeacians . . . ';[3] and Calypso says, 'I shall not give him safe-conduct in any way. For I have no ships with oars nor companions that could take him over the broad back of the sea.'[4] This means that by divine decree the compulsive covering which hides Odysseus away from the world he knows and that knows him is to be lifted only gradually and under hardship. He has to travel alone, on a vessel built by his own hands, and no god will protect him. Calypso does what she can for him, equipping him with all necessities, sailing instructions and a fair wind.[5] But within sight of Phaeacia the wrath of Poseidon returning from the Ethiopians strikes him, and he would have been lost in the storm but for the help of the sea-nymph Leucothea. When he swims ashore at last on Scheria he is naked and at the end of his strength.

In Phaeacia there is also a wish to retain Odysseus, but it is gentle and delicate and soon withdrawn. While Calypso is one who conceals and holds back, the Phaeacians are people who 'conduct travellers home safely and without disaster';[6] and their ships, who have a mind of their own and need no helm to direct them, travel wrapped in mist and cloud; and there is never any fear of damage or disaster for them.[7] It is on one of these ships that Odysseus three days after his arrival is carried home to Ithaca, bedded comfortably, sleeping a deep sweet sleep. When Poseidon's wrath strikes again, it turns the ship as it approaches Scheria into rock, but Odysseus is safe on the shore of Ithaca.

The two episodes of Ogygia and Phaeacia are contrasted in another way still: by the figures of Calypso and Nausicaa. Calypso is a mighty goddess. She wants Odysseus to be her husband, and for ever tries to charm him with gentle and flattering words.[8] While she cannot prevent him from grieving on the shore during the day, he must spend the night with her 'unwillingly with her willing'.[9] There is no doubt that she loves him. She saved his life when he was cast ashore after Zeus had split his ship with a thunderbolt and his companions had perished.[10] She cared for him, and she also promised to 'make him deathless and unageing for ever'. When Hermes brings the order from Zeus that she must let him go she shudders,[11] and she is bitter and angry that the gods begrudge her this man, as they have done with other divine women. But she has to obey—and then makes the best of the situation. For she does not mention Zeus' command to Odysseus but speaks of her own kindly willingness and mercy.[12] She comes to the hub of the matter when after dinner she once more puts before Odysseus the alternatives between which he has to choose: a journey home full of sorrows, or immortal life at the side of Calypso, even though he desires to see his wife for whom he longs all the days.[13] But Calypso is incomparably superior to Penelope, a goddess to a mortal. Odysseus humbly acknowledges this, but it makes no difference: he wants to go home however great the perils of the journey.

Here the poet represents the greatest obstacle to Odysseus' return to Ithaca (he stays seven years!): a mature woman who loves him, a goddess who offers immortality, who can also keep him by force. Odysseus has enjoyed her love for a time,[14] but in the end he rejects Calypso and all she has to offer, out of his loyalty for Penelope and his longing for home.

On Scheria the woman who might test his loyalty is Nausicaa, a maiden rather than a woman, mortal, but a wealthy king's daughter, with the beauty of a goddess and surrounded by a happy people who spend life in seafaring devoid of danger and in games, dancing, music and poetry. The freshness, delicacy and humour with which Homer represents the thoughts and feelings of this girl about marriage and about the godlike hero who has so strangely come to her shores has often been described.[15] What is perhaps not so well known is how this is wrought into the carefully constructed episode of Phaeacia. The theme of Nausicaa's possible marriage to Odysseus is set into a sad and lovely counterpoint with the theme of Odysseus' safe-conduct home. Stirred by Athene's words in her dream Nausicaa goes to wash her family's clothes with the thought of her approaching marriage in her mind. As she does this, Odysseus appears. Addressing her he praises her parents and her brothers as blessed in having her, but most of all her future husband;[16] and he wishes her the fulfilment of all her wishes, a husband, a house, and perfect harmony in her married life. When Odysseus is washed, and beautified by Athene, Nausicaa wishes that such a man might be called her husband, and that it might please him to stay in Scheria.[17] Her instructions to him are lit up by her hopes as she asks him not to accompany her, but to follow her into town later in order to avoid awkward gossip. But at the same time she speaks seriously of the safe-conduct home that her father and mother may provide for him.[18] When Odysseus has told Alcinous and Arete of his journey from Ogygia to Phaeacia, and how Nausicaa clad him, Alcinous is annoyed with his daughter for not bringing the stranger to him herself, but Odysseus, lying tactfully in order to protect the girl from her father's anger, says that he himself was afraid of annoying the Phaeacians and refused to accompany the princess. Alcinous is delighted, and wishes that a man like Odysseus would marry his daughter. He offers him a house and possessions if he were willing to stay. But he goes on to say immediately, 'But no-one among the Phaeacians will keep you back against your will!',[19] and he offers him safe-conduct home. Odysseus joyfully accepts the offer. Nothing is said about Nausicaa, but Odysseus is understood and his decision accepted.

A brief exchange of farewell between Nausicaa and Odysseus closes the episode in Book 8. Odysseus meets the young princess as he goes into the hall for dinner. In two brief lines Nausicaa wishes him well and asks him to remember her when he is home, since she has saved his life.[20] Odysseus answers, in four lines, that Zeus might give him safe homecoming, and that there he would pray to her like a goddess, because she saved his life. This is the end of Nausicaa's brief hopes about the stranger and Odysseus' final temptation to stay away from Ithaca.

The poet has chosen to tell the episodes of Calypso and Nausicaa himself in direct and full narrative, because the journey from the one to the other represents for Odysseus the dramatic transition from being 'concealed' on a distant island as a prisoner to the people whose ship will take him home.

## A Hypothesis about the Origins

In the wanderings of Odysseus one can distinguish between the materials which have been used and their possible origins on the one hand, and what has been fashioned out of these materials on the other.

If we consider the materials of Odysseus' adventures, there is much that gives the impression of actual geographical localities and actual seafaring. I do not intend to take sides in the controversy about the detail of this matter. For my purpose it is sufficient to say that personal experience and hearsay about voyaging in the Mediterranean and perhaps the Black Sea has certainly gone to the making of Odysseus' adventures. But there is also another side to these adventures which make them appear as folktales or fairy stories. Let us review the elements which one might describe in this way, and see whether together they may suggest something about their origin.

From Ismarus, land of the Cicones, comes the overwhelmingly potent wine which dopes the Cyclops.[21] The lotus of the Lotus-eaters is a strange food which is so delicious that it makes people want to stay and eat it and forget all about everything else.[22]

The Cyclopes are man-eating, one-eyed giants.[23] The Laestrygonians are also man-eating giants. Their land where the paths of day and night are close together is to the north.[24] The Phaeacians are not giants, but they used to live in the 'Upper Land', close to the giants.[25] Through friction with the Cyclopes they emigrated to Scheria which is far away from humans, furthest away in the sea, unvisited by mortal men.[26] But the great-grandfather of Alcinous, king of the Phaeacians, was Eurymedon, king of the giants. Furthermore, the Phaeacians, like the Cyclopes and the giants, are close to the gods.[27] That is why the gods used to visit the Phaeacians undisguised, and even in the present do not conceal themselves when they meet a solitary Phaeacian wayfarer on the road. What is striking here is that the Cyclopes, the Laestrygonians, and the Phaeacians are all giants or descendants of giants, and that they as a group are said to be close to the gods. In addition, the Cyclops who is blinded by Odysseus is a son of Poseidon;[28] and Poseidon is also the grandfather of Alcinous, king of the Phaeacians.[29] Moving among these various Beings Odysseus therefore moved in a region close to the gods.

Aeolus is the 'steward of the winds' by Zeus' decree.[30] Circe is the daughter of the Sun, and granddaughter of the Ocean,[31] and her island is situated where there is the house and the dancing-place of early-born Dawn and the Rising of the Sun.[32]

The forbidden cattle which the foolish companions of Odysseus slaughter belong to the Sun.[33] Finally, there is the entrance to Hades in the sunless region of the Cimmerians.[34] Wind, Sun, Ocean and Underworld (practically the four elements) are cosmic forces or regions. When Odysseus comes to meet Aeolus, Circe and the spirits of Hades on his travels, he seems to visit the various spheres of the cosmos, even though he is travelling by ship and on the horizontal all the time.

We have already mentioned that the land of the Laestrygonians must lie to the north, because there the paths of day and night are close together. The sunless land of the Cimmerians is also northern, of course. Circe is a sister of Aeetes, who was the father of Medea and king of Colchis on the East coast of the Black Sea. This and the reference to the ship Argo and to the Clashing Rocks point to the north-east and, as Meuli has shown, to a tradition from which the later *Argonautica* derived.[35]

To sum up, the folktale elements in Odysseus' wanderings have the following common features: Odysseus moves in a world which is beyond the world of man, among Beings who are close to the gods, and others who are related to the various spheres of the cosmos both above the earth and within the earth. Moreover, there are a number of references to the north or north-east. The question is whether a common origin for these features can be found.

The distinction which the Chadwicks have drawn between 'heroic' and 'non-heroic' in oral literature relating to specified human individuals is relevant here. They say: 'We have usually divided the material into "heroic" and non-heroic". The former is literature normally—not invariably—concerned with persons of princely rank—their exploits, adventures and experiences. The latter is most commonly concerned with seers, sages and saints, and their intellectual and spiritual achievements and experiences; but we have also included under this head literature relating to other persons, chiefly princes, if the object of such literature is to illustrate doings or experiences of spiritual interest.'[36] About the relationship of these two classes of oral poetry they say: 'They are seldom or never wholly uninfluenced by one another. Heroic themes (Type C) come to be cultivated in non-heroic circles, and non-heroic themes, or at least elements from such themes, penetrate into heroic circles. Commonly the tendency is for the non-heroic to encroach upon the heroic.' With reference to the Homeric poems, they state that these belong to the sort of 'heroic poetry which is unaffected, or very slightly affected, by non-heroic influence', 'except *Od*. IX-XII';[37] in fact, the wanderings of Odysseus. If we ask the question what, if anything, in these wanderings is 'heroic poetry' as described by the Chadwicks, the answer is: only the very first one, the raid on the Cicones, a piratical raid characteristic of a heroic warrior.[38] The rest is non-heroic poetry, that is poetry which, according to the Chadwicks, is concerned with the intellectual and spiritual achievements and experiences of seers, sages, saints or princes. But the 'seer' of the north and north-east, to which the above-mentioned references in the wanderings point, is from the point of view of Greece the shaman. Karl Meuli has placed the wanderings of Odysseus, at least in part, into this context.[39] He makes it plain that he does not regard the Odysseus of *our Odyssey* as a shaman. But he believes that behind the figure of Odysseus in our *Odyssey* an older figure appears reconstructed in the work of scholars like Hartmann, Bethe and Schwartz from traditions outside the Homeric epics. This older figure was, according to Meuli, closely connected with a journey into the Beyond and a consultation of the dead. He also believes that the narrative form of the wanderings, namely in the first person, is derived from the ancient shamanic tradition. At the end of his paper, however, Meuli warns in a footnote against an unwarranted extension of the notion of 'shamanism' to cover a great deal that is similar, but does not really belong to the northern, Eurasian 'shaman', strictly speaking. Since then Mircea Eliade has in his comprehensive book on shamanism[40] brought out clearly the essential features of the northern shaman, paying attention also to similar or related phenomena. On the basis of his work it is now possible to test and fill out Meuli's theory of shamanic elements in the Odyssean wanderings.[41]

A shaman is a person who is set apart from other persons, and acquires special powers by his initiatory experiences in

which he receives his vocation. Men of this sort form a 'small
mystical elite' among the people for whom they work.[42] The
source of the shaman's power is an experience of ecstasy, 'a
trance during which his soul is believed to leave his body and
ascend to the sky or descend to the underworld'.[43] It is by
means of such a trance that a shaman cures the sick, accom-
panies the spirits of the dead into the underworld, and medi-
ates between his people and the gods and spirits of the
Beyond, whether of the heavens or the underworld. During
his ecstatic journey the shaman drums on his ceremonial
drum; he dances, and sings songs in which he describes what
he sees and experiences: the road, rivers, mountains, the
spirits of the dead and much else. Arriving back on earth he
tells of his adventures.[44] In his songs the shaman may use
a traditional poetic diction which is rich in vocabulary,[45] but
he always sings *ex tempore* so that each performance produces
a new creation, though achieved with traditional means, precisely as oral epic is produced even today in Yugoslav as
Milman Parry and A. B. Lord have shown.[46] In these shamanic performances we have one of the main sources of oral
epic. As Eliade puts it, 'When we attempt to evaluate the
cultural contribution of shamanism we shall show to what an
extent shamanic experiences contributed toward crystallizing
the first great epic themes.'[47]

On this background, I shall attempt to show that the
'scheme', as it were, of a shamanic journey is still discernible
in the wanderings of Odysseus; and further that certain
details may also be explicable by reference to a tradition in
which shamanic material was incorporated.

Why should Odysseus arrive in Ithaca asleep? Telemachus
and Theoclymenus sit up during their night journey to
Ithaca.[48] But Odysseus' sleep is no ordinary sleep. As the
Phaeacian rowers churned up the sea with their oars, 'sweet
sleep drooped upon his eyelids, a sleep from which one is not
easily wakened, very sweet, most closely alike unto death.'[49]
Odysseus did not even waken when the Phaeacians carried him
from the ship and laid him down on the shore of Ithaca. I
suggest that this sleep may be a remnant left in the story
of a shaman's trance.[50]

If Odysseus' arrival in Ithaca in his sleep and his awakening there may originally have been the *end* of a trance, the question should be raised whether there is any trace of the *beginning* of this trance, a trace which one would expect to find at the beginning of his tale at the court of Alcinous. From Troy Odysseus and his companions sailed to Ismarus, land of the Cicones, in Thrace. Although this is out of the way for someone travelling from Troy to Ithaca, it is intelligible as an act of piracy for the purpose of gaining treasure and as an act of vengeance against allies of Troy.[51] But Ismarus in Thrace becomes significant for our question when we add the information which Homer supplies a little later in connection with the Cyclops episode. When Odysseus with twelve of his companions sets out for the cave of the Cyclops, he takes with him a goatskin full of black sweet wine which Maron, son of Euanthes, priest of Apollo, who was the protecting deity of Ismarus,[52] gave him. Maron gave it to Odysseus, because he had kept him, his child and his wife safe, out of reverence, since he lived in the grove of Phoebus Apollo. Together with seven talents of gold and a silver mixing-bowl the priest gave him twelve jars of this wine, sweet and undiluted, a divine drink. Its existence was kept secret; only his wife and one maid-servant knew of it. When they drank of it, they mixed one part of it with twenty parts of water. It was so potent; potent enough to put to sleep even a giant like Polyphemus.

There are in this tale two features that suggest connection with shamanism: the priest of Apollo, and his miraculous wine.

Apollo is the god of the Greek pantheon who was connected with shamans of the Greek world.[53] Aristeas from Proconnesus on the Sea of Marmara, 'was seized by Apollo', and carried off to the land of the Issedones.[54] Abaris was called a Hyperborean,[55] and the Hyperboreans were closely connected with the Apollo of the north.[56]. Pythagoras was called 'Hyperborean Apollo' by the people of Croton in southern Italy.[57] 'Orpheus neglected the worship of Dionysus' for Apollo, as Guthrie says.[58] Shamanic figures like Aristeas, Abaris and Pythagoras were of course, and Thracian Orpheus may have been, later in date than Homer. All the same, the traditions about them contain characteristics of shamans who were in touch with the Greek world, and are valid for inferring an earlier state of affairs.

The connection between Apollo and the miraculous wine is strange. Apollo is not usually connected with wine. The typically Greek connection of ideas appears later in the Cyclops of Euripides where Maron, the giver of the wine, is called the son of Dionysus. But on an Etruscan mirror which belongs to the end of the fifth century B.C. in a style rooted in the Greek art of the second half of the fifth century, the seer *Chalchas* is represented as an elderly man with long wavy hair on head and beard but thinning above the brow, and with two mighty wings sweeping along the whole length of his back. He examines a liver which he is holding in his hand.[59] Behind him stands a wine-jug.[60] Here *Chalchas,* who is a priest of Apollo according to the *Iliad,*[61] is winged because his prophecy arising from his study of the liver in front of him takes him on a spiritual journey. The jug suggests that the seer has used wine as a stimulant to ecstasy.

The motif of the wine may not have been older than the eighth century. But the story of Apollo and his priest Maron or whatever he was called may well have contained, instead of 'wine', the motif of a 'narcotic' strong enough to make a person fall into a trance. The shamans certainly used narcotics of various sorts in order to induce ecstasy.[62] But even though such a narcotic may be shamanic in origin, its original shamanic function is both obscured and superseded. The wine is used to put Polyphemus to sleep, not Odysseus. But at the point where Odysseus' trance would have begun, that is, after the meeting with Maron, Odysseus is first struck by a storm from the north and then driven off course at Cape Maleia. From this point on, all Odysseus' adventures have elements of the extraordinary and miraculous in them. This does not exclude the localities of these adventures from being definite geographical places. On the contrary, such a realism is in complete harmony with Homer's handling of shamanic motifs as we shall see. 'Being driven off course' is what in the *Odyssey* has superseded the beginning of trance and the beginning of an ecstatic journey to the Beyond.

To sum up, Apollo and the miraculously potent wine together point to a shamanic context.

One of the most important purposes of a shaman's journey is to escort the spirit of a dead person down into the world beyond and to settle him there.[63] Just before Odysseus leaves for the Underworld, the youngest of his companions sleeping upstairs in a drunken stupor is roused by the din of his friends making ready to start. He forgets that he is on the roof, falls straight down, and dies of a broken neck. His ghost approaches Odysseus as he sits at the mouth of the Underworld waiting for Tiresias, holding his sword over the trench filled with sacrificial blood. Elpenor comes, because 'he had not yet been buried under the broad-pathed earth';[64] and because his body is not buried, he cannot yet join the spirits of the dead, but is still able to speak to Odysseus without drinking of the blood. Elpenor explains to Odysseus, who is surprised to see him, what has happened, and begs him for honourable burial on his return to Circe. Odysseus promises to fulfil his wishes. When he returns to Circe's island he buries Elpenor exactly as he had asked him to do. We know that the spirit of the dead man is now at peace in the Underworld.

While the shaman escorts such a spirit into the Beyond, Odysseus meets at the opening of the Underworld a companion who has just died and by his promise and subsequent burial appeases him. The Greek belief that the dead are settled and pacified by burial is substituted for the shaman's activity as an escort of the dead. At the same time, a natural death and burial is aesthetically a satisfying frame for Odysseus' journey to the dead, an idea which Virgil in *Aeneid* 6 has used and expanded.

The place where Odysseus stays longest, in fact seven years out of the ten years of his wanderings, is Ogygia, the island of Calypso.[65] This island is connected with the 'navel of the sea'.[66] Calypso is the daughter of destruction-minded Atlas, who knows the depths of all the sea and himself holds the mighty pillars that keep heaven and earth apart.[67] This is a significant group of mythological images which need interpretation.

*Omphalos* means the 'navel' of a human body and the central boss of a shield. It is not clear whether the island is at the navel, that is at the centre of the sea, or whether it itself *is* the navel of the sea.[68] Whichever it is this island is central to the sea. The idea of the 'centre' plays an important part in the shamanic picture of the cosmos. Eliade describes this cosmos as follows:[69] 'There are three great cosmic regions, which can be successively traversed because they are linked together by a central axis. This axis, of course, passes through an "opening", a "hole"; it is through this hole that the gods descend to earth and the dead to the subterranean regions; it is through the same hole that the soul of the shaman in ecstasy can fly up or down in the course of his celestial or infernal journeys.' The cosmic axis is then at the 'centre' of the cosmos. About the idea of the 'centre', Eliade says that it is not necessarily cosmological, but may be any sacred place in which some 'transhuman presence' from the sky or from below has made itself felt. The island of Calypso is at the 'centre' of the sea in this sense.[70] That it is at the centre of the sea rather than the earth or the world is in keeping with the fact that all Odysseus' travels are by ship and over the sea.

The name of Calypso's island is most fitting for a place which has the holiness of being a 'centre' in the world: it is Ogygia. The word does not occur elsewhere in Homer. It means 'primeval' or 'primal'. Hesiod, for instance, uses it to describe the 'imperishable water' of Styx by which the gods swear an oath that binds even them under threat of terrible punishment.[71] The name Ogygia denotes then the awesome 'originality' of this island.[72]

Calypso's father is 'evil-minded Atlas, who knows the depths of all the sea, and himself holds the mighty pillars which hold heaven and earth apart.'[73] This picture of Atlas is composite. A simpler version is found in Hesiod's *Theogony*: 'The son of Iapetus (*i.e.* Atlas) holds the broad sky, standing up straight, with his head and tireless arms'.[74] Here it is the person and body of Atlas himself who with his head and arms supports the sky, and this is the representation of Atlas which we find in sculpture and painted on vases.[75] The combination of pillar and the person of Atlas found in our Odyssean passage occurs also in Aeschylus' *Prometheus* where he 'stands propping up the pillar of heaven and earth with his shoulders'.[76] Elsewhere the name of Atlas is given to a mountain. Herodotus mentions a Mount Atlas somewhere near the North African shore: 'It is narrow and rounded in all directions, and it is said to be so high that one cannot see the summit, since it is never free of clouds in winter or summer. The native people say that it is the pillar of the sky'.[77] R. W. Macan in his commentary on the passage says: 'This description of Mount Atlas in no respect corresponds to the local facts.' This suggests that the idea of the 'sky pillar' has determined the description of the mountain.[78] Pindar calls Mount Aetna a 'sky pillar'.[79] In Greek thought Atlas bearing the sky, the pillar bearing the sky, and the mountain bearing the sky, all express the same idea. Occasionally two of these pictures are combined, as when Atlas 'props up the pillar of heaven and earth' in the *Prometheus*. In our Odyssean passage we find the same combination, only further complicated, because there is more than one pillar holding earth and heaven apart. In later Greek thought, Atlas was directly identified with the World Axis.[80]

Now the idea of the central axis of the world forms, as we have seen, part of shamanic cosmology. The mythical images which express this idea vary: it may be seen as the 'Pole Star, holding the celestial tent like a stake', the Pole Star being called 'Sky Nail' by some, and 'Nail Star' by others.[81] Often the tent pole is assimilated to the Sky Pillar and receives sacrifices like a god. Another image for the central axis is the 'Cosmic Mountain'. The Tatars of the Altai for instance imagine their highest god 'in the middle of the sky, seated on a golden mountain'.[82] This image of the World Mountain, however, occurs also in Near Eastern and Indian thought. While it is merely part of a picture of the cosmos, it is not particularly shamanic. But when the shaman climbs this Pillar or Mountain, then this image becomes part of a personal, mystical and ecstatic experience, and the World Axis, whether seen as Sky Pillar, Mountain, or World Tree, for that matter, forms an essential part of the shamanic journey into the

Beyond.[83] In the *Odyssey,* Odysseus in person arrives at the island of the daughter of Atlas. In the *Odyssey* this motif is therefore shamanic rather than of a more general Eastern provenance.

To return to our Odyssean passage, Atlas is then originally the Sky Pillar or Cosmic Mountain conceived in the personal form of a strong hero. The description of Atlas as 'destruction-minded' is intelligible now, because the approach to this Being would certainly be dangerous: the shaman's ascent of the Sky pillar or the Cosmic Mountain towards the heaven is fraught with danger.

Atlas is also described by Homer as he 'who knows the depths of all the sea'; he is envisaged, according to Stanford, 'as a giant with his head in the clouds and his feet deep in the sea'.[84] A connection of Atlas with the sea is also expressed in Hesiod's genealogy where the mother of Atlas is Clymene, daughter of Ocean.[85] In Indian mythology, the gods use the Cosmic Mountain to stir up the primeval ocean with it.[86] On the centre of the shamanic drum of the Transbaikal Tungus are drawn 'eight double lines' which 'symbolize the eight feet that hold the earth above the sea': [87] here there is sea below the earth, and the central axis must be imagined as piercing both sea and earth.

Again, the fact that Odysseus stays on Ogygia for seven years may be significant in relation to shamanism.[88] The most frequent figures for the superimposed heavens through which the shaman ascends to the highest gods are seven and nine.[89] The Cosmic Pillars of the Ostyak, for instance, have seven incisions. As Eliade says,[90] 'The mystical number 7 apparently plays an important role in the shaman's technique and ecstasy, for among the Yurak-Samoyed the future shaman lies unconscious for seven days and seven nights, while the spirits dismember and initiate him; the Ostyak and Lapp shamans eat mushrooms with seven spots to enter into trance; the Lapp shaman is given a mushroom with seven spots by his master; the Yurak-Samoyed shaman has a glove with seven fingers; the Ugrian shaman has seven helping spirits; and so on.' The importance of the number 7 is not original in shamanism: it has come into Central and North Asian shamanism from the ancient Near East. Since again Odysseus' sorrowful stay of seven years on Ogygia is the personal experience of an individual hero, it corresponds to the shaman's experience of ascending through the seven heavenly planes: the figure 7 is therefore more likely to be derived from northern shamanism than directly from the Near East. Two other pieces of evidence support this. First, the shaman Aristeas reappeared in the seventh year after he had left behind his body as if dead in the city of Proconnesus.[91] Secondly, the Pleiades are called daughters of Atlas by Hesiod,[92] and the number of stars in the constellation of the Pleiades is seven.

The image of the 'World Tree' has already been mentioned as being exchangeable in shamanic thought with the Sky Pillar or the Cosmic Mountain. Two further ideas connect with the World Tree which are relevant to our investigation. When the shamanic novice on his journey of initiation reaches the centre of the world, he finds on the summit of the Cosmic Mountain the World Tree. By the will of the 'Universal Lord' he receives from the tree the wood from which he makes his shamanic drum, the 'vehicle' of all his ecstatic travelling.[93] The symbols with which the shaman's drum is identified are many: it may be the shaman's 'horse' on which, as he drums, he rides up to the sky.[94] It may be a 'stag' or a 'roebuck'.[95] It may be called 'bow' or 'singing bow', being used like a stringed instrument, the music or song being the vehicle of his travel.[96] The arrow sent off from the bow may also be an image of the shaman's ecstatic journey.[97] Among the Transbaikal Tungus, 'the shaman uses his drum as a boat to cross the sea',[98] so that among the pictures on his drum he has representations of the shores to which his boat takes him. This complex of mythical images has its correspondences in our Odyssean passage. Only once in the whole of the *Odyssey* does a decree of Zeus, who is the 'Universal Lord' of the Greek Pantheon, directly affect Odysseus. For Zeus sends Hermes to the island of Ogygia to command Calypso to let Odysseus go 'on a much-roped ship', but with no escort from gods or men.[99] Hermes takes the message to Calypso, who acts on it. She takes Odysseus equipped with axe and adze 'to the furthest part of the island, where grew mighty trees,

alder and poplar and fir reaching to the sky,[100] long ago sapless
and dry which would quickly float for him'.[101] From this tim-
ber Odysseus makes his much-roped boat. The command of
the highest god, the great trees, and the boat made with wood
from them: this is a shamanic group of motifs, but they
have become more realistic and thoroughly Greek.

Finally, Eliade says of the World Tree that it 'becomes a
tree of Life and Immortality as well. Enriched by innumer-
able mythical doublets and complementary symbols (Woman,
the Wellspring, Milk, Animals, Fruits, etc.) the Cosmic
Tree always presents itself as the very reservoir of life and
the master of destinies'.[102] The daughter of Atlas, who is, as
we have seen, equivalent to the Sky Pillar and the World Axis
and so also to the World Tree—the daughter of Atlas is
Calypso. She lives in a cave which is surrounded by a flour-
ishing wood of alders, poplars and sweet-scented cypress trees.
All sorts of birds have their nests in it. Around the mouth
of the cave grows a vine hung with grapes. Five springs of
clear water flow from it in various directions, and round
about are meadows full of the bloom of violets and water-
parsley.[103] Indeed a place of fertility and abundance! In the
midst of all this lives Calypso, who wants Odysseus to be her
husband[104] and offers to make him 'deathless and unageing
for ever'.[105] The position of Calypso is here precisely the
position of the Teleut shaman's 'celestial wife' who lives in
the seventh heaven. I will quote the Teleut shaman's meeting
with his celestial wife in full: 'During his ecstatic journey to
Bai Uelgaen (*scil.* the highest god), the shaman meets his
wife, and she asks him to remain with her; she has prepared
an exquisite banquet for them. "My darling young kam! (she
sings)./We shall sit together at the blue table . . ./My darling
husband, my young kam,/Let us hide in the shadow of the
curtains/And let us make love to one another and have fun,/
My husband, my young kam!" She assures him that the
road to the sky has been blocked. But the shaman refuses to
believe her, and repeats his determination to continue his
ascent: "We shall go up the 'tapti' (the spiral groove cut in
the shaman tree)/And give praise to the full moon"/(an
allusion to the stop that the shaman makes on his celestial

journey to venerate the Moon and the Sun). He will touch no food until he has returned to earth. He calls her "My darling, my wife", and adds: "My wife on earth/is not fit to pour water on thy hands" '.[106] Calypso, having received Zeus' command, takes Odysseus home to dinner.[107] After the meal she once more offers the prize of immortality to him if he will stay with her and she points out how inferior Penelope is to herself in beauty. Odysseus acknowledges this but wants to continue his journey, like the Seleut shaman. At the conclusion of the chapter, Eliade himself mentions Calypso and Odysseus.

Calypso and all the mythical images that cluster round her seem, then, to be shamanic in origin. The name of Calypso is Greek, of course, and means the 'Concealer', the woman who wants to conceal this man from everybody else and keep him on her island at the navel of the sea far away from gods and men. The name suits her role as the 'celestial wife' very well. It is quite possible that Homer invented it, though it may be older in the bardic tradition.

To sum up this first part of our investigation, we have encountered motifs which are probably shamanic in origin at four different points in the wanderings of Odysseus, that is in Books 5 to 13.187: (1) the potent wine given to Odysseus by Maron, priest of Apollo, at Ismarus, city of the Cicones, and Odysseus being driven off course at Cape Maleia; (2) Odysseus' meeting with Elpenor in the Underworld; (3) Odysseus' stay with Calypso, daughter of Atlas; (4) Odysseus returning to Ithaca asleep. These motifs or groups of motifs probably derive from a shaman entering into trance, conveying the spirit of a dead person into the Underworld, travelling to the World Axis to ascend to the sky or descend into the Underworld and return from there, and the end of the trance. The importance of these motifs is still evident in Homer. Odysseus' stay with Calypso lasts seven years out of the ten that pass for him between Troy and Ithaca. The Ciconian adventure is the first in the series, and the deep sleep on the Phaeacian ship is the last, forming the transition to Ithaca. The visit to the Underworld is marked as important by the central place it takes in Odysseus' tale about his wanderings.[108]

For, roughly speaking, it is preceded by six adventures and
followed by six. It is preceded and followed by a stay with
Circe. Finally, this book is divided into two parts by the only
interruption when Alcinous once more promises safe-conduct
home and rich guest-gifts. In all probability then, the 'scheme'
of Odysseus' wanderings is derived, as a whole and also in
some detail, from a shaman's ecstatic journey into the Beyond.

For further confirmation of this hypothesis, I will compare
the wanderings of Odysseus with the Journey into the Beyond
of Parmenides. W. K. C. Guthrie says about the prooemium
of Parmenides: 'The general character of the prologue points
rather to the "shamanistic" strain in early Greek religious
thought, represented by semi-legendary figures like Aithalides,
Aristeas, Abaris, Epimenides and Hermotimus.'[109] Hermotimus
used to search for knowledge on his spiritual journeying,[110]
and Epimenides 'encountered the goddesses Truth and
Justice'.[111] About Parmenides' prologue Guthrie says that 'what
is here described reads like a similar spiritual journey "above
the earth" with knowledge as its goal.' Since it is extremely un-
likely that Parmenides living about 450 B.C. thought of
Odysseus' wanderings as in any way shamanic, his poem
stands in a shamanic tradition quite independently of Homer,
so that comparable features would confirm our hypothesis.[112]

The mares drawing the chariot of Parmenides correspond
to the raft or ship on which Odysseus sails, and particularly
to the Phaeacian ship which carries him in his death-like sleep
to Ithaca.[113] While in several passages the Phaeacian ships
seem to travel like other ships,[114] in his speech to Odysseus
Alcinous says the following: 'Tell me your land and people
and city in order that the ships may take you there directing
their course with their mind. For the Phaeacians have no
steersmen or rudders which other ships have. But the ships
themselves know the thoughts and minds of men, and they
know the cities and rich fields of all men, and swiftly travel
over the gulf of the sea wrapped in mist and cloud; nor is
there for them any fear of harm or destruction.'[115] These
ships that know the cities and lands of all men and have minds
to guide their own course are akin to the 'wise' mares that
set Parmenides 'on the far-famed road of the god (*i.e.* the

Sun), which bears the man of knowledge over all cities'.[116]

The text of Parmenides goes on: 'On that road was I borne, driven on both sides by the two whirling wheels, as the daughters of the Sun, having left the house of Night, hastened to bring me to the light, throwing back the veils from their heads with their hands.' They come to the Gates of Night and Day, and persuade Dike to open them, and pursue their path until they come to the Goddess, who receives the traveller graciously and gives him knowledge. The daughters of the Sun have a close parallel in Circe who is a daughter of the Sun god[117] and whose island is located by the house of Dawn and the rising of the sun: [118] by her advice she guides Odysseus on his travels into the Underworld,[119] and after his return from there past the Sirens, the Planctae, Scylla and Charybdis and Thrinacia.[120]

Finally, the Sirens offer knowledge to him who listens, just as the Goddess gives knowledge about truth and falsehood to Parmenides. But for Circe's warning, Odysseus' voyage past the Sirens would have been the finish of his homecoming and also of his life. For whoever approached them out of ignorance and heard their song did not return home to wife and children.[121] But sitting on a meadow they sang their spellbinding song, surrounded by the bones of dead men. In addressing Odysseus the Sirens themselves explain the nature and content of their song in order to entice him: their voices speak with the sweetness of honey, and will delight him; and he will acquire knowledge. For they know all that happened before Troy, and in fact all that happens on the earth.[122] The lure of their song lies then in its sweetness and in the knowledge about past and present which it offers.

It is astonishing to realize that this is precisely the power of the Muses, and consequently the power which Homer himself hopes to exert as the instrument and servant of the Muses. Introducing the Catalogue of the Ships in the *Iliad* the poet appeals to the Muses, saying, 'For you are goddesses, and you are present, and you know everything, but we only hear what is said, and know nothing (*i.e.* by immediate experience).'[123] He wants help with the enumeration of the leaders

of the Greeks and their ships: there were so many that even
if the poet had ten tongues and ten mouths, an unbreaking
voice, and a heart of bronze, he could not do it without the
help of the Muses to aid his memory. Here the gift of the
Muses is much concrete detail about events of the past, in
fact about the people active in the Trojan War about which
the Sirens know everything. The spell cast by the singer's
tale over his listener is represented in a simile by which
Eumaeus describes the beggar Odysseus telling his tale: 'Just
as when a man gazes at a singer who having learned from the
gods sings lovely tales to men, and they desire incessantly to
listen to him whenever he sings, thus he (Odysseus) bewitched
me sitting beside me in the house.'[124] The word *thelgo* means
both 'I bewitch' and 'I charm and delight'. The victims of
the Sirens are like men spellbound by a singer whose tale
does not end until his listeners have died listening. Odysseus
hears the song of the Sirens. But on Circe's advice he is
fettered to the mast of his ship, and through these bonds
escapes the power of the 'Binders'.[125] In the *Odyssey* the
Sirens are an obstacle to Odysseus' return, just as the other
Beings are that he encounters. All the same, what they offer
to their listener is knowledge, and this is what Parmenides
receives from the Goddess beyond the Gates of Night and
Day, and this is what Hermotimus and Epimenides seek on
their spiritual journeys. Again a shamanic motif is used but
its function is changed.

The nature of the Sirens in post-Homeric tradition is also
important for our hypothesis. However difficult it is to determine what sort of Beings they really are, particularly in the
seventh and sixth centuries when they are frequent in representative art, they always belong to the World of the Beyond
wherever the context is clear. Ernst Buschor distinguishes
between the Sirens of fairy tale, *Märchensirenen,* and the
'Muses of the Beyond'.[126] The first are the Sirens of the
*Odyssey* and whatever follows that tradition. The others are
spirits of the Beyond, part bird, part human, who are connected with the dead, mostly in the Underworld, but also in
the heavenly regions.[127] If our hypothesis about the wanderings
of Odysseus is correct, the Sirens of the *Odyssey* are originally

no different from the later Sirens: namely, Beings of the World of the Beyond.

Finally, the question must be asked at what period shamanic material entered the body of heroic tradition originating from Mycenaean times. Only one thing is certain, namely that Homer did not himself take this material out of a shamanic context. The extent to which, as we have seen, shamanic motifs are changed, displaced, or altered in function suggests that the 'shamanic journey' became part of bardic tradition long before Homer.[128] This opens up two possibilities. It may have come in during the period of migrations, the Dark Age. It has been argued that this was a formative period in the development of Greek oral epic.[129] E. R. Dodds connects the appearance of shamans like Aristeas, Abaris, Pythagoras and Orpheus with Greek trade opening up the Black Sea in the seventh century and in this way bringing Greeks into contact with the Scythians whose shamanism has been fully described by Meuli.[130] But Thracian shamanism[131] might well have been known to the Greeks earlier. It is not hard to see how shamanic material could have become attached to an originally Mycenaean hero, Odysseus in particular: Odysseus and the shaman share a powerful intelligence and the capacity to speak well.

On the other hand, the shamanic material may go back to the Mycenaean Age. It is possible that some of the Mycenaean nobles practised 'shamanic journeying' themselves. E. A. S. Butterworth has suggested this for Agamemnon;[132] and W. Burkert believes that the sacrificial table, knife, and so on, found in a Mycenaean cenotaph at Dendra on the Peloponnese may witness to shamanistic rites for the purpose of laying at rest the spirit of one who had died far away without burial.[133]

In conclusion, we may say with some probability that in the wanderings of Odysseus the poet used material ultimately derived from a shaman's journey into the Beyond. The ancient 'scheme' of such a journey is still discernible; and a number of themes can be connected with shamanic ideas. This is as far as diachronic investigation can go: we cannot find out how the shamanic journey and its various motifs were developed and altered as bard after bard took them over and sang them anew. But we can explore synchronically the final result, namely Books 5 to 12 of the *Odyssey* as we have them. In all his adventures, Odysseus encounters obstacles to his return home which he overcomes. We have seen earlier, at least to some extent, how the poet has shaped these adventures: they are arranged in such a way as to make Odysseus' stay with Calypso and with the Phaeacians the ground and basis for all the others.

# CHAPTER III

# GUEST - FRIENDSHIP

The social institution of guest-friendship forms part of the material with which Homer works. In the action of the *Odyssey* it is one of the most important themes and occurs many times over. The situation which calls for guest-friendship is always this, that a stranger arrives at the entrance of a house and has to be received. This situation is bound to occur frequently in the *Odyssey,* since Telemachus is travelling in strange places in Books 3 and 4, Odysseus in Books 5 to 12, and Odysseus comes to the hut of Eumaeus and then to the Ithacan palace as a stranger in the second half of the epic.

M. I. Finley[1] has described guest-friendship as a social institution which can be seen to be functioning in various parts of the *Odyssey*. This description is made by bringing together relevant incidents, and abstracting from them the nature and functioning of this institution. I shall briefly summarize some of Finley's results.

Guest-friendship is not merely a matter of sentiment, but a practical relationship. It still existed in the sixth century B.C. when, according to Herodotus,[2] envoys of Croesus, King of Lydia, and the Spartans 'took the oaths of guest-friendship and alliance'. Here guest-friendship becomes political alliance between nations; in Homer it is always a relationship between individuals. The ground and origin of this institution is the fact that the relationship to the stranger moved between two extremes: fear, suspicion and distrust on the one hand, and

friendship and generosity on the other. Finley speaks of 'the
basic ambivalence of the heroic world toward the uninvited
stranger' and 'the oscillation between deep, well-warranted
fear and lavish entertainment'.[3] The very word *xenos* implies
this ambivalence: it means both 'guest-friend' and 'stranger'
or 'foreigner'. An instance of lavish entertainment of a
stranger is of course Odysseus' reception by the Phaeacians.
An instance of the flouting of the obligations of guest-friendship is the behaviour of the Cyclops whose 'guest-gift' to
Odysseus is the promise that he will eat Odysseus last! This
is *hybris,* and the Cyclops is punished by losing his sight.
Generally in the world of Odysseus a guest-friend is an
'effective substitute kinsman, protector, representative and
ally'.

The duty of guest-friendship falls on everybody, but parti-
cularly on a king.[4] In Book 17, Odysseus goes round the
Suitors begging for food. He also comes to Antinous, and says:
'Give, friend! You are in my eyes not the worst of the
Achaeans, but the best, for you are like unto a king. Therefore, you must also give better than the others of food and I
shall spread your fame over the boundless earth.'[5] When
Antinous refuses to give him anything, beggar Odysseus says:
'Alas, you have then the beauty but not also the mind. You
would not even give salt from your household to a person
begging, since you give nothing from another man's wealth.'
The implication is, of course, that it is easier to be generous
with someone else's property than one's own. When Odysseus
says this, he means that Antinous looks like a king, but does
not have the outlook of a king. Antinous, who desires the
kingship of Ithaca, understands this and replies by hurling
a stool at him. This scene makes it plain that kingship implies
generosity in giving, and this is what makes a king famous.

In addition, guest-friendship implies good manners.[6] The
stranger must not be kept waiting. He may be offered a bath
and fresh clothes: the 'foot-washing' that Penelope offers to
the beggar is part of such hospitality, as she says herself.[7]
The main item of hospitality is of course a meal.[8] After the
meal, *not* before, comes the question: who are you? and
what is your need? This sequence is explicitly mentioned by

Telemachus, by Nestor, by Menelaus and by Eumaeus;[9] and it is in fact what happens. Before a guest leaves, he is offered or given a guest-gift,[10] an institution which keeps its force even when it is mocked, as by the Cyclops or by Ctesippus.[11] In the end, the stranger is given safe conduct to wherever he wants to go, if he needs it.[12] Finally, the stranger is under his host's protection as long as he is in his house.[13]

Guest-friendship as a social institution within the texture of Greek life is taken for granted by the poet. It probably formed part of the poetic tradition with which he worked, and also part of his own life and the life of his audience, while we moderns have to reconstruct it in order to be able to share as far as we may the poet's presuppositions. For the poet it was a matter of how he could use this institution or theme as a theme in his composition. We must therefore now take the further step of finding out what he did with it. For this purpose we will compare the poet's presentation of hospitality as it is offered to Telemachus first by Nestor and then by Menelaus, and as the Phaeacians offer it to Odysseus.[14]

Nestor is making public sacrifice to Poseidon with his people early in the morning on the beach when Telemachus and Athene arrive. Menelaus and his people are celebrating a double wedding in his palace in the evening when Telemachus and Pisistratus arrive. Odysseus' arrival among the Phaeacians is two-fold. He first meets Nausicaa on the beach in the morning when she has washed clothes and played with her maids; he first meets the royal pair in the evening in their palace among their nobles. The alternation between morning and evening, beach and palace is hardly fortuitous. At Pylus the strangers are received eagerly and immediately, especially by Pisistratus. At Sparta Eteoneus hesitates to admit the strangers whom he sees at the gate, and only does so when he is scolded for his remissness by Menelaus. Nausicaa is immediately willing to give Odysseus what hospitality she can on the beach. But Alcinous and Arete are so taken aback by the sudden appearance of the suppliant Odysseus that they sit in silence until old experienced Echeneus admonishes Alcinous to raise the suppliant from the ashes of the hearth and offer him hospitality. This he does of course with great generosity.

Here again the poet has alternated between two ornamental themes; immediate reception and hesitation combined with admonition. At Pylus a bath and fresh clothes are not mentioned during the day that Telemachus and Athene spend with Nestor on the beach. But before Telemachus leaves the palace on the next day, he is bathed, anointed, and clothed by Polycaste, Nestor's youngest daughter. At Sparta, Telemachus and Pisistratus are bathed, anointed, and clothed by maids of the palace, as soon as they arrive, and before the meal. Nausicaa, meeting Odysseus on the beach, tells her maids to bath him in the river and to give him a meal. But Odysseus wants to wash himself, and he does, oils himself, and puts on the clothes given to him. The motif of the clothes given to the stranger is used further in Book 7, when Arete recognizes them as belonging to her own household and asks about them.

The description of the meal is most specific for Pylus where it is a great sacrificial feast: eighty-one bulls are slaughtered for an assembly of four thousand five hundred people. First the entrails such as heart, liver and spleen are eaten, while the thigh-bones are burned for the god. After prayers to Poseidon, the flesh of the beasts is roasted and eaten. At Sparta the meal is introduced by a formulaic passage about hand-washing and serving of the food, and by a speech of Menelaus inviting his guests to eat and praising their noble appearance. The meal is brief and largely formulaic. Odysseus' meal on the Phaeacian beach is extremely brief; in the palace it is introduced by five of the seven formulaic lines of Book 4. The meal itself takes one line, and is followed by a drink-offering to Zeus. But in Book 8 Alcinous provides a great public feast in honour of the guest, enhanced by the song of the bard.

The most interesting variety of ornamentation occurs in relation to the question directed to the stranger about who he is, where he comes from and what his need is. In Pylus, Nestor asks the question, and Telemachus answers it quite simply. In Sparta, Menelaus mentions Odysseus without as yet being aware of Telemachus' identity. Telemachus weeps. Both Helen and Menelaus believe that they can recognize in him the son of Odysseus, and Pisistratus confirms their belief.

Here the question is neither asked nor directly answered by the person concerned. Instead a new theme is introduced, namely 'recognition'. This is ornamental here in the sense that it functions as an expansion to the theme of 'Who are you?' and its answer. In the second half of the epic it becomes one of the main compositional themes. The question of what Telemachus stands in need of is asked by Menelaus the next morning and is answered by the tale of Menelaus' wanderings.

Among the Phaeacians this theme of question and answer about the stranger's identity is ornamented in the most spectacular fashion. It spans in fact Books 7 to 12. In the evening, before the Phaeacian nobles retire from the palace, Alcinous proposes that in the morning they will entertain the stranger and prepare to take him to his home; then he suggests that the stranger might be a god.[15] This is an indirect question about Odysseus' identity. Odysseus replies that he is not a god but a wretched mortal with more misfortunes to tell than any other. He wants to be left in peace to eat and drink. So he gives no answer. When the nobles have left, and Odysseus is alone with the royal pair, Arete asks three questions: 'Who and whence are you? Who gave you these clothes?'[16] Odysseus answers by describing his voyage from Calypso to Phaeacia and how Nausicaa gave him the clothes. This is of course only a very partial answer to the question 'Whence?' and none at all to the question 'Who are you?'

Book 8 opens with a public assembly of the Phaeacians in the early morning in which Alcinous makes arrangements for taking the stranger home. When he mentions 'this stranger here', he adds, 'I do not know who he is.'[17] There follows the most lavish entertainment. After dinner Demodocus sings his first song. Its theme is the quarrel of Odysseus and Achilles. Odysseus weeps as he hears it and Alcinous, noticing this, suggests a different form of entertainment: games out in the open. After contests of running and wrestling, Odysseus is challenged to compete in stone-throwing. Roused to anger he wins the contest, and then speaks of his craft with bow and arrow, a passage which foreshadows the death of the Suitors. Alcinous turns to lighter matters: there is dancing, the Song of Ares and Aphrodite, dancing again and more guest-gifts.

With night falling, the company returns to the palace. Arete produces a chest in which all the gifts are placed and which Odysseus fastens with a complicated knot taught him by Circe. After a welcome bath he goes to join the diners, when he meets Nausicaa for the last time. In two brief lines she wishes him well and asks him to remember her when he is home, since she saved his life. Odysseus answers (in four lines) that Zeus might give him safe homecoming and that there he would pray to her like a goddess, because she saved his life. This is the end of Nausicaa's brief hopes about the stranger and Odysseus' final temptation to stay away from Ithaca. At the dinner which follows, Odysseus honours the singer and asks for the song of the Wooden Horse. Again Odysseus weeps; and again Alcinous notices it and takes matters in hand. This time he once again promises safe-conduct, and then asks for Odysseus' name and homeland.

It is plain from the structure of the book that the three songs of Demodocus are related to each other. The song of the Quarrel at the beginning and the song of the Wooden Horse towards the end are sung in the palace, each one followed by tears of Odysseus. The latter song describes the end of the Trojan War through the Wooden Horse, a piece of guile invented by the resourceful Odysseus, and Odysseus' victory over Deiphobus, then husband of Helen. By asking for this song himself, Odysseus is beginning to disclose who he is.

The first song, the song of the Quarrel between Achilles and Odysseus, is a counterpiece to it.[18] It connects both with the beginning of the war and with the end of it: 'For at that time the beginning of pain rose up like a mighty wave towards the Trojans and the Greeks through the counsel of great Zeus.'[19] It was then that Agamemnon went to Delphi to consult the oracle of Apollo. Homer does not say what he asked, but as Marg points out,[20] it is plain that being the leader of an army he would consult the god about the outcome of the war. Later, when Odysseus and Achilles fell out, Agamemnon was delighted that the best of the Achaeans quarrelled, no doubt because in the oracle such a quarrel had been connected with the conquest of Troy. Since the conquest of Troy celebrated in Demodocus' third song was brought about by the guile of Odysseus, it is probable that in this dispute at an earlier state in the story Odysseus advocated guile in some form. Odysseus' supreme intelligence in guile and trickery is, of course, a theme which runs right through the *Odyssey*.[21] Achilles, on the other hand, is in the bardic tradition a man who hates guile. In the ninth Book of the *Iliad* he replies to the speech of Odysseus (which is not guileful, but at any rate a speech of 'resourceful' Odysseus) that he will speak out freely so that no-one may murmur against him: 'For he is hateful to me like the gate of death who hides one thing in his mind, and says another.'[22] But Achilles' supreme fighting power is acknowledged everywhere in the *Iliad*. The obvious conclusion from all this is that the quarrel between Achilles and Odysseus was concerned with the superiority of either force or guile.[23] The first song of Demodocus therefore prepares for his third song in which Odysseus' guile triumphs.

The second song of Demodocus is quite different from the other two, both in tone and subject matter. It is sung outside, in between dances. It tells of some of the gods in a light and humorous vein; and it delights Odysseus instead of making him weep. While the other songs are much abbreviated, this story, brief though it is, is told in full, both in action and dialogue. The subject is a love affair between Ares and Aphrodite, wife of Hephaestus. Hephaestus, the husband, is told of it by the Sun and fashions unbreakable but also invisible fetters which he fits around the conjugal bed. Then he departs. Ares immediately proceeds to make love to Aphrodite and the pair is enmeshed in the fetters. Hephaestus returns and calls all the gods to witness. Laughter and bantering follow, until Hephaestus, on a promise of payment of a fine, releases the culprits, who hurriedly escape. The content of this song is adultery caught in the act and its punishment. The adulterer is the handsome swift-footed God of War, who is vanquished by the lame, but clever, husband Hephaestus. The comment of the gods sums up the tale: 'Evil deeds do not prosper. The slow man catches the swift. Thus even now Hephaestus being slow has caught, though he is lame, by his craft Ares who is the swiftest of the gods that inhabit

Olympus; therefore he owes him the fine for adultery.'[24] No wonder that Odysseus was delighted with this song: in terms of a divine comedy it foretold the triumph of his own intelligence over the Suitors who were wooing his wife, as Tiresias had told him in the Underworld.[25]

If we now look at the three songs of Demodocus in sequence, we realize that in them the poet reveals and praises, step by step, Odysseus as a mighty intelligence: first contrasted with Achilles, strongest fighter of the Greeks, then under the image of Hephaestus with Ares, the War-god himself, and finally victorious over Troy by the device of the Wooden Horse. In the end it is Alcinous the king himself who asks Odysseus directly who he is;[26] and Odysseus replies, not only telling him his name and home but the whole story of his wanderings from Troy (Books 9 to 12). Here the traditional question of the host to his guest about who he is is ornamented so lavishly as to be built up through two whole books (7 and 8), and the answer of the guest-friend Odysseus covers four books (9 to 12).

The theme of the guest-gift is also ornamented, though less fully. Nestor is deprived of the chance of giving something to Telemachus, because the young man passes Pylus by on his return journey.[27] Menelaus promises splendid gifts: three horses and a chariot and a beautiful mixing-bowl, but Telemachus asks for treasure only, as Ithaca is too mountainous for a chariot.[28] When Telemachus leaves Sparta in Book 15, Menelaus gives him a silver cup with a rim of gold, given to him by the king of Sidon, and Helen a dress for his future bride, made by the queen's own hand.[29] Among the Phaeacians guest-gifts are mentioned first by Alcinous who asks for a cloak and chiton and for a talent of gold from each of the twelve kings of Scheria.[30] He hicself provides a handsome chest for the gifts, cloak and chiton and a golden drinking-cup and, delighted by Odysseus' tale of his wanderings, he adds tripod and bowl from each of the kings, a most splendid gift.

In these books the theme of guest-friendship has been ornamented with great wealth. In fact ornamentation with variety and contrast is the principle of composition here, as in many other instances in the *Odyssey*. We shall further see that Homer also makes dramatic use of guest-friendship in the presentation of several of his characters, in particular in the development of Telemachus.[32]

# CHAPTER IV

# TESTING

Whether testing a person is, like guest-friendship, a social institution in the Homeric world, it is difficult to ascertain; it is certainly a recurrent theme in the *Odyssey*, with a clearly patterned sequence. In order to describe this sequence we must compare several instances of testing in the poem and abstract from them their common pattern. The situation in which testing a person or making trial of a person arises is this: after ten years of the Trojan War, and in some cases more years of wanderings, the king of the land returns home. One such king, Agamemnon, is murdered by his wife and her lover who has usurped the kingship.[1] In the Underworld Agamemnon therefore warns Odysseus not to return openly, but in disguise; and Odysseus returns as an old dirty beggar. From the security of this disguise he explores the lie of the land: he tests the members of his household, that is, the members of his own family, his retainers and his slaves. The question asked, or more often implied, is this: 'Are you still Odysseus' friend, and will you fight for him?' This question can only be asked in safety as long as Odysseus is unrecognized. If the answer is in the affirmative, and if the time is ripe, Odysseus may reveal his identity. Then the person tested in turn proceeds to test Odysseus in order to find out whether Odysseus is really the man he says he is. There are then two types of testing: Odysseus coming home tests the loyalty of those at home (type 1); and those at home test the truthfulness of Odysseus regarding his identity (type 2). All this forms of course part of the major theme of 'recognition'. Testing of the first kind precedes recognition; testing of the second kind follows it, and confirms it.

The simplest form of testing occurs in Book 21.[2] All the Suitors except Antinous and Eurymachus have tried in vain to string the bow of Odysseus. At that point, the cow-herd Philoetius and the swine-herd Eumaeus leave the hall, and the beggar Odysseus follows them. Outside in the courtyard he speaks to them with winning words: 'Cow-herd and you, Swine-herd, might I say a word or shall I keep it back? But my spirit tells me to speak out. What would you be like in helping Odysseus if he arrived from somewhere quite suddenly, and a god brought him? Would you fight for the Suitors or for Odysseus? Tell me how your heart and spirit command you.' Philoetius replies by a prayer to Zeus that Odysseus might return; and Eumaeus adds his own prayer. Having recognized their true mind Odysseus reveals himself and before they can even ask the question he gives them a 'clear sign' so that they might 'recognize him well and be persuaded in their heart'. The sign is the famous scar on his thigh.[3] There follows a brief scene of delighted recognition, and then Odysseus gives instructions to the loyal men for the imminent battle, particularly about bringing the bow to him. The phases of this very condensed scene of testing are the following:

1 Odysseus hesitates whether to ask the question about loyalties or not;
2 Odysseus asks for whom the two men will fight, Odysseus or the Suitors (type 1);
3 The reply is: for Odysseus;
4 Odysseus reveals himself;
5 Odysseus gives them the sign of the scar to convince them (type 2 testing is implied, though owing to the brevity of the scene not executed);
6 Joy and lament of recognition;
7 Move into action.

These seven or so phases are characteristic of other scenes of testing.

*Phase 1*—Odysseus has in mind to kiss and hug his father,

and then wonders whether he should test him first; he decides
on the latter.[4] Menelaus wonders whether to let Telemachus
speak of his father himself or whether to ask and test everything first.[5] Before he can decide, Helen acts for him. There
is also one example of this initial hesitation in connection with
the second sort of testing: Penelope, who has been told that
Odysseus is back and has slain the Suitors, wonders whether
to ask her husband from a distance or to go up to him and
kiss him.[6] She tests him first.

*Phase 2*—The simple question of Book 21 about loyalty
(type 1 testing) is ornamented fully and with great variety.
Odysseus tests the swine-herd's generosity by a clever fictitious
tale in which he is saved from freezing to death in an ambush
before Troy by Odysseus, who calls for a volunteer to run to
the camp for reinforcements; the man who volunteers leaves
his coat behind and the shivering man is saved. The swine-
herd is pleased with the tale and promises all the beggar needs
for the night.[7] Once again Odysseus tests Eumaeus to see
whether he would offer further hospitality or whether he
would urge him to go to town. So Odysseus suggests that he
will go to the palace and beg there, and that he might even
act as a servant to the Suitors. How provocative this sugtion is becomes plain from Eumaeus' reply when he answers
'with great agitation' that he will die at the hands of the
ruthless Suitors if he goes without protector, and that he must
stay where he is.[8] The element of provocation evident in this
scene is a motif which is richly developed in Odysseus' testing
of Penelope and of Laertes, scenes which will be described in
detail later.[9]

*Phase 3*—The response to the test may be a simple action,
such as producing a warm coat or the offer of further hospitality in the case of Eumaeus, or a furious onslaught of abuse
and threats in the case of the maid Melantho.[10] It may be
an illuminating description of the situation and an outburst of
genuine grief for the lost husband or son, and a new readiness
to act, in the case of Penelope and Laertes.[11]

*Phase 4*—If the moment is right Odysseus reveals his identity.

*Phase 5*—As we have seen he proves it by showing his scar to the two herds before they even try to test his truthfulness (type 2 testing). But Laertes asks Odysseus to tell him a clear sign so that he may believe; and Odysseus mentions the scar and also definite numbers of fruit trees which Laertes gave him as a boy.[12] Penelope, hesitating first whether to test Odysseus,[13] then proceeds to provoke Odysseus into revealing the 'great sign': she orders Eurycleia to prepare a bed for Odysseus outside the bed chamber. Odysseus replies with much agitation.[14] He had himself fashioned their marriage bed, making the trunk of a live olive tree into one of the bed posts; and Penelope's order makes him afraid that the trunk might have been cut and the bed moved. Thus Penelope forces Odysseus by a provocation that even Odysseus cannot resist to prove who he is, and then flies into his arms convinced at last that she will not be deceived. Earlier, Penelope had tested the beggar for his truthfulness in his account of entertaining Odysseus in Crete; and the beggar had described the clothes of Odysseus, his finely-wrought brooch and his personal herald, which all were recognized as signs by Penelope.[15]

*Phase 6*—When recognition is thus made certain and all danger of deceit is eliminated, the reunion is enjoyed with tears and delight.

*Phase 7*—Finally, the reunited people move into action together. The two herds follow Odysseus into the hall to play their part in the bow contest and the battle. Laertes will share the final battle with his son and grandson, while Penelope will keep quiet and look after the possessions of Odysseus and the house until the war is over.[17]

It is clear that testing a person is a well-established compositional theme in the *Odyssey*. Its ornamentation varies from instance to instance, but the underlying pattern is always discernible. The most extensive examples of testing will be described in the chapters on Odysseus and Laertes.[18]

To return to the question whether 'testing' is also a social institution, Peter G. Katzung in his dissertation on 'The "Testing" in the Action of the *Iliad*'[19] comes to the following conclusion: when Agamemnon says he will 'test' the Achaeans 'with words' he intends to find out exactly what the situation and the attitude of the Achaeans to it is, and furthermore and more importantly to change their attitude from the apathy that he expects to a new eagerness to fight. Both these elements are in evidence in the *Odyssey* in Odysseus' testing of Penelope and Laertes. The testing scene in the second book of the *Iliad* is then another instance of the compositional theme we have discussed. What is more, Agamemnon says, 'I will test them as it is the righteous custom (*themis*).'[20] Katzung defends this translation of *themis* by a general reference to the second half of the *Odyssey*. Our analysis of the theme of testing, together with this line from the *Iliad*, makes it highly probable that testing was indeed a social institution.[21]

# CHAPTER V

# OMENS

Omens and their interpretation are a religious institution found everywhere in ancient Greece throughout its history. In the *Odyssey* the interpretation of omens is a craft which has its own conditions and its own procedure.

An omen may be interpreted by a professional seer, such as Halitherses[1] or Theoclymenus.[2] Or it may be interpreted by a lay person, such as Helen, when the gods themselves impart such knowledge. She says: 'Listen to me! I will prophesy to you, as the immortal ones throw it into my heart, and as I believe it will be fulfilled.'[3]

The art of prophetic interpretation of omens itself involves two steps. Halitherses is introduced in this way: 'he alone excelled among those of his own age by recognizing birds and pronouncing fateful things.'[4] The first step is the recognition of a bird as a divine omen. For, as Eurymachus says: 'many birds fly under the rays of the sun, and they are not all fateful.'[5] The second step is the interpretation of the omen with reference to the person whom it concerns.

There is a variety of types of omens in the *Odyssey*: bird omens, whether actual birds or birds appearing in a dream, chance remarks[6] which are overheard and bode well for the listener, a sneeze, and mightiest of all the thunder of Zeus.

The bird omens, which are the most complex, are remarkable for their regular structure. The omen itself consists, in each case, of the action of one or more big birds of prey, which in all but the first omen is an act of violence done to smaller birds. In each case, an indication of place points to the person with reference to whom the omen must be interpreted. In Book 2 the two eagles swoop down towards the heads of all those assembled, glaring destruction, and they fly through their houses and city.[7] This makes it plain that Zeus' punishment will befall the assembly, which is, of course, led by the Suitors, and the whole city. Halitherses' interpretation takes careful account of these features when he says that this omen concerns the Suitors in particular,[8] but also many others throughout Ithaca.[9] It is surprising, however, that he does not seem to take any notice of there being two eagles when he says: 'for Odysseus will not be long absent from his loved ones.' It is an act of discretion on the part of Halitherses when he does not say that Odysseus and Telemachus will be preparing destruction for the Suitors together, while in fact the picture of the two aggressive eagles foreshadows the picture of Odysseus and Telemachus fighting the Suitors side by side, in Book 22. In Book 15 the local indications are ambiguous.[10] The eagle snatches up the goose from the yard of Menelaus' house, but it then comes close to the chariot of Telemachus and swoops past in front of it and to the right. This twofold local reference to the house of Menelaus and the chariot of Telemachus causes Pisistratus to ask Menelaus whether this sign is meant for Telemachus himself or for Menelaus. Helen, inspired by the gods, decides. In Book 19 the omen takes place in the house of Odysseus, so that the reference is not in doubt.[11] The omen in Book 20 is very short, and its reference is expressed very simply: 'and to the left of them (which means: boding evil for them, *i.e.* the Suitors) came a bird, an eagle . . .'[12]

Each omen is preceded by a wish, whether actually expressed or implied in word or action. In Book 2 Telemachus prays to Zeus for vengeance on the Suitors, and the omen represents the god's assent.[13] In Book 15 Telemachus wishes that he might find Odysseus at home and that he could tell him about the generous hospitality he has received from Menelaus.[14] The omen indicates fulfilment. In Book 19 Penelope has opened her heart to the stranger, the burden of her speech being that, longing for Odysseus, she consumes her heart.[15]

When she has gained confidence in the stranger's truthfulness, she once again tells him of her great grief[16] and then of her terrible uncertainty whether still to stay or whether to go and marry another man. It is plain from what she has said before that it is her heart's wish to stay and wait for Odysseus; the bird omen of her dream justifies her in this, though she does not believe the dream to be true. In Book 20 'the Suitors then were preparing death and fate for Telemachus.'[17] The wish to kill Telemachus is, of course, implied in this; the omen, being on the left, denies fulfilment of this wish.

These omens are then preceded by a wish to which the gods accede fulfilment if the bird is on the right and deny fulfilment if it is on the left. The omens also contain a local indication of the person or persons to whom the omen refers.

The third omen is difficult in detail, and particularly interesting, because it is interpreted twice in different contexts.[18] Telemachus suggests to the fugitive seer Theoclymenus that he will find hospitality in the house of Eurymachus, who is 'by far the best man and most eager' to marry Penelope and obtain the kingship of Odysseus.[19] He concludes: 'but Zeus of Olympus who dwells in the aether knows whether he will before the wedding accomplish for him (Eurymachus) the evil day.'[20] The wish implied here is, of course, that Eurymachus might die before marrying Penelope. Apollo, sending his messenger the hawk on the right, promises fulfilment of this wish. It means that the dove whose feathers the hawk is tearing out is Eurymachus. Who is the hawk? This is indicated by the fact that the feathers fall to the ground between the ship which Telemachus has led and Telemachus himself. The feathers, which are the symbol of the imminent destruction of Eurymachus, fall into the realm of power of Telemachus. In this way they point to Telemachus being intended by the hawk, Telemachus not necessarily as an individual, but as a representative of his *genos*. As Telemachus' words have made it plain that the issue between Eurymachus and himself is the kingship of Ithaca, Theoclymenus interprets the omen accordingly: 'no other line is more royal than yours among the people of Ithaca, and you will always be the stronger.'

Two further features merit attention. Theoclymenus introduces his interpretation by saying that he has recognized this
bird as being an omen sent by a god.[21] Thus his prophecy
proceeds in professional manner according to the two steps
discussed above. Furthermore, the question has been raised
why Theoclymenus takes Telemachus aside, away from his
companions, to tell him his prophecy.[22] Theoclymenus is a
stranger, and he must not be presumed to know any more
about the situation in Ithaca than what Telemachus has told
him or what the god might tell him in an omen or a vision.
In consequence, Theoclymenus does not know whether Telemachus' companions are loyal to him, or to what extent
Telemachus has to hide his aspirations to the throne of Ithaca.

The same omen of the hawk carrying off the dove and
tearing its feathers is interpreted once again by Theoclymenus,
this time to Penelope.[23] In the meantime, he has been staying
with Piraeus, Telemachus' friend, and is no doubt fully
acquainted with the situation in Ithaca. When Penelope, Theoclymenus and Telemachus meet together, Penelope asks Telemachus with intense urgency whether he has heard anything
about his father's homecoming.[24] Telemachus' news is meagre:
Nestor knew nothing, Menelaus only that Odysseus was held
by Calypso on an island.[25] At this point the seer comes in. He
calls Zeus and the hospitable table and hearth of Odysseus
to witness to the truth of his prophecy: 'indeed Odysseus is
already in his own country, finding out about these evil deeds
here whether he is sitting idle or on the move, and he is
"planting" evil for all the Suitors. Such was the bird omen
which I observed sitting by the well-benched ship and told Telemachus.'[26] Odysseus is finding out the evils that are being
done 'whether he is sitting idle or bestirring himself'. A
similar alternative occurs in Helen's prophecy: 'Odysseus
will come home and exact punishment, or he is already at
home, and plants evil for all the Suitors.'[27] Here Odysseus'
homecoming is in accord with Telemachus' wish,[28] but is as
yet unfulfilled, though it will be fulfilled in the end. In the
case of the omen for Penelope the alternative is even more
pointed. Up to this moment Odysseus is sitting quietly in
Eumaeus' hut, but very shortly[29] we hear how Odysseus and

Eumaeus set off for the town, how Odysseus encounters evil Melantheus, and soon at the palace Antinous and the rest.

We have here the remarkable fact that one bird omen is interpreted twice over, in each case for a different person, and differently, according to the practice demonstrated above that a bird omen either grants or denies fulfilment to someone's wish that precedes it. Thus the first time Theoclymenus prophesies in accordance with Telemachus' wish that Eurymachus, his rival in his striving for the kingship, should die; the second time, in accordance with Penelope's wish to hear of the homecoming of Odysseus. So he says first: 'your line will be the superior royal line for ever', and then, 'Odysseus is here planning destruction to the Suitors.' In practice, the two prophecies come to the same, of course: Odysseus' presence and victory will save his own kingship and that of his son.

Omens and their interpretation are then a clearly defined institution in the world of the *Odyssey*. We shall see presently how the poet uses them in relation to his characters, in particular in relation to the seer Theoclymenus.

But he also uses the bird omens as a sequence of significant images moving to a climax within the course of the whole. The first omen[30] consists of two eagles flying together over the assembly and city of Ithaca; they glare destruction upon the assembled Ithacans, and they are full of grief, clawing their own cheeks and necks, but they have as yet no victim.[31] The second omen is an eagle snatching up and carrying off a white goose; the great bird has seized his prey, but does not hurt it yet.[32] The third omen is a hawk carrying off a dove and tearing out its feathers; he will soon kill it.[33] The fourth omen which occurs in a dream is an eagle breaking the necks of twenty geese; and the eagle is Odysseus himself.[34] This is the climax, which is immediately followed by Penelope's resolve to institute the shooting contest which will of course result in Odysseus killing the Suitors. The fifth omen is like an epilogue. An eagle appears to the Suitors carrying a trembling dove.[35] But this wish picture is not fulfilled: the bird comes on the left. We see the poet here constructing his work with exquisite precision.[36]

If finally we consider all the omens in the *Odyssey* together, a striking fact emerges concerning the distribution of the various types of omens over the various recipients. An omen consisting in a person's words is granted to Telemachus and Odysseus, the sneeze to Penelope, the bird omens to Telemachus, Penelope and the Suitors, the fourth one to Odysseus together with Penelope.[37] But no one except Odysseus receives as a sign the thunder of Zeus. Zeus thunders when on the morning of the day of vengeance Odysseus prays for a sign. He thunders when Odysseus draws the bow. Finally he throws a thunderbolt to stop Athene and Odysseus from fighting on.[38] It is plain that no one else stands in such close relationship to Zeus as Odysseus. This connects with the kingship of Odysseus: it is Zeus who makes a man into a king.[39]

# PART II

# THE PEOPLE IN THE ODYSSEY

## CHAPTER VI

# THEOCLYMENUS

Theoclymenus is the great seer of the *Odyssey*. His appearance in Book 15 at the point when he is needed in the economy of the epic is carefully prepared for earlier.

Without being mentioned by name, a noble seer is spoken of in Book 11, in the catalogue of heroines.[1] One of the heroines whom Odysseus sees is Chloris from Minyan Orchomenus, wife of Neleus, king of Pylus. She bore three sons, the oldest of whom was Nestor, and one daughter, Pero. The story of her marriage is told in a highly condensed form and is not completed. Being a marvel to men, she was wooed by all the young men living in the neighbourhood: an epic theme, of course, which is fully developed in the *Odyssey*. As in the *Odyssey*, the Suitors were pitched against one another in a contest which in this case was instituted by the maid's father. Neleus was willing to give his daughter only to the man who would steal the cows of Iphiclus from Phylace. We are not told why Neleus demanded this trial rather than any other. It was certainly difficult, and the only one prepared to try it was a 'noble seer': 'A noble seer alone promised to drive them out.' The fact that he 'promised' to steal them suggests that he did not intend to marry Pero himself if he was successful. To whom he made the promise we are not told. In the undertaking he ran into trouble through the harsh ordinance of a god: cowherds caught him, and he was imprisoned for a year. Iphiclus set him free on account 'of his prophecies', 'and Zeus' will was being fulfilled': presumably in all that happened

to the seer, and perhaps also to Iphiclus. Here the tale stops.
It began with Pero and her Suitors and ends with the 'noble
seer', who is set free after a daring exploit because of his
power of prophecy. The contest of the Suitors is left unfinished. The image of the great seer remains.

In Book 15 Telemachus is approached by a seer who is
fleeing from Argus, because he has committed a murder.[2] He
is a descendant of Melampus who previously lived in Pylus.
As the story proceeds—again in a highly condensed manner,
though differently—we realize that the 'noble seer' of the
catalogue was Melampus, and that his story is told once again.
We have no means of knowing whether Homer's audience
realized in Book 11 that Melampus was meant. Whether or
not, the nameless mention in Book 11 certainly would arouse
interest and curiosity.

Melampus had been a rich man, resident in Pylus. But he
emigrated to another land to escape from Neleus. Then the
story moves into the past, in the characteristic 'appositional'
manner, in order to explain this.[3] Neleus had previously by
force seized and kept many possessions of his for a year.
This was during the year when Melampus was a prisoner in
the house of Iphiclus on account of Neleus' daughter, and on
account of the infatuation which a divine Erinys had put
into his heart. But he escaped from death, drove the cattle
from Phylace to Pylus, took vengeance on Neleus, gave Pero
in marriage to his brother, and himself emigrated to another
land, to Argus where he lived as the lord of many Argives,
married and had children. This story begins a little earlier than
the story in Book 11, gives more detail, completes the account
of the wooing of Pero, and then leads further. Melampus is
said to be a very rich man in Pylus, which at least suggests
reasons for Neleus' act of robbery, although we are only told
the fact. The wooing of Pero is not mentioned again directly
but only as the cause of Melampus' imprisonment. The description of Melampus' action in relation to Pero as 'infatuation',
put into his heart by Erinys, is new, and is an expansion on
11.292-3. The brief phrase, 'but he escaped from destruction',
summarizes the account in Book 11, where his release by
Iphiclus was explained by his prophetic activity. The story

in Book 15 moves on beyond that of Book 11: he drove the cattle to Pylus—which makes one wonder about his relationship to Iphiclus—and married Pero to his brother. This concludes the story of Pero's wooing, which had been left unfinished in Book 11. It is now clear that in 11.291 Melampus promised his brother that he would try to win Pero for him. Why the intention or desire to do this should be called *ate*, and be due to Erinys, we do not know. Melampus took vengeance on Neleus for his robbery (in what way we do not know), and then—presumably because after this it was no longer safe for him to stay in Pylus—he emigrated to Argus.

While in Book 11 the story ended pointedly where the prophetic power of Melampus comes to the fore, this is not even mentioned in Book 15. On the contrary, the story is told partly more briefly, partly more fully, as we have seen, as an explanatory expansion on the fact that 'he then went into the land of other people', which is picked up after the expansion by 'he went to the land of other people',[4] namely, horse-feeding Argus.

The mention of Argus reminds us of the seer who was descended from Melampus and who was fleeing from Argus. From this point on the story of Melampus becomes a genealogy. He had two sons, Antiphates and Mantius. The grandson of Antiphates is Amphiaraus, beloved of Zeus and Apollo, which refers to his greatness as a seer. His untimely death and its causes are alluded to, and two sons of his are mentioned. One of the two sons of Mantius is Polyphides, whom Apollo made the best prophet among men when Amphiaraus had died. And this man's son was Theoclymenus.

First of all then, the story of the Suitors' contest for the hand of Pero and of Melampus' part in it, is full of detail, alluded to rather than properly told. This makes it highly probable that it was part of the bardic repertoire at the time of Homer.[5] If this is so, we must ask why Homer brings this story into the *Odyssey* twice, each time very briefly and elusively. The first time the story comes in as a tale about Pero, beautiful daughter of the heroine Chloris; and to this extent it is firmly imbedded in the catalogue of the heroines in the underworld. But Homer points beyond this by stopping with the mention of the seer's prophetic powers—by not telling the end of the seer's exploit and return to Pylus, and also by not mentioning the seer's name. We are left to expect the name and the tale of the great seer.

The second time the story is told in connection with a seer who is a descendant of Melampus, and who will turn out to be the great seer of the *Odyssey*. It is told with new detail and brought to its conclusion, but it is so elliptical that without its first version in Book 11 it would be quite unintelligible, which makes it certain that the two forms of this story were composed in such a way as to fit together and complement one another. The function of the story of Melampus' exploit for the sake of Pero was different in the second form. It is no longer necessary to praise Melampus' power of prophecy; that has been done in Book 11. But it is desirable to show why Melampus emigrated from Pylus to Argus, for it is from Argus that his descendant Theoclymenus is fleeing. The reason for this change of home of Melampus is told as part of our story in this version of Book 15: he had to flee from Neleus. The function of the genealogy is to show that the great seer Melampus gave rise to a line of great seers: Amphiaraus was his great-grandson, Polyphides his grandson, and Theoclymenus was the son of Polyphides.[6]

It is then plain that the two passages about Melampus form a highly wrought introduction of almost gorgeous splendour to the appearance of the fugitive suppliant Theoclymenus.

Theoclymenus, fleeing from Argus because of manslaughter, asks Telemachus with great anxiety who he is, because, pursued as he is by men who want to kill him, he is in danger whenever he speaks to an unknown person.[7] Telemachus tells him his own position and takes him on his ship. It is on behalf of Telemachus that Theoclymenus uses his prophetic powers first of all: he interprets the omen of the hawk tearing the dove on their arrival in Ithaca.[8] Thereby he conveys to Telemachus the will of the gods that his house shall be supreme in Ithaca; and he himself gains access to the hospitality of Odysseus' home.

Next Theoclymenus prophesies to Penelope. The meeting of Penelope with Theoclymenus is carefully constructed. When

Telemachus returns to the palace, Penelope receives him with great joy and asks eagerly for his news.[9] But Telemachus tells her to have a bath, put on clean clothes, and to pray to the gods vowing sacrifices, if Zeus will grant retribution. He himself will go and fetch Theoclymenus. Why does Telemachus deal so harshly with his mother? Because his own news from abroad is disappointing: Nestor knew nothing, Menelaus only that Odysseus was alive, but with no means of coming home; and the real and great news of Odysseus' being in Ithaca he is bound by Odysseus' command not to tell her.[10] But he trusts that the seer will. Therefore Telemachus goes to fetch him at once. After bath and dinner, Penelope asks once again, this time petulantly, if not angrily, about news of Odysseus' homecoming. Now Telemachus tells her how Nestor knew nothing, and Menelaus only that Odysseus was alive, but a prisoner on an island. At this point, Theoclymenus breaks in, and prophesies the very presence of Odysseus in Ithaca. Penelope answers, full of hope and gratitude. Clearly, Theoclymenus' prophecy is intended to come as a climax to Telemachus' tale of his journey.[11]

Theoclymenus prophesies a third time, this time to the Suitors foretelling their doom, and Odysseus himself is present. They are already out of their minds by Athene's power, laughing with tears in their eyes, eating meat running with blood. Theoclymenus' prophecy is the most eery passage in the whole *Odyssey*.[12] It is a prophetic vision which describes the Suitors wrapped in night, sighs flaming, cheeks tear-stained, walls and beams spattered with blood, the whole house full of ghosts going into the Underworld, the sun lost out of the sky, and an evil fog over it all. The Suitors laugh sweetly, and think the seer is mad. He leaves them as men doomed.[13]

Theoclymenus plays the role which his elaborate introduction foreshadows. He prophesies to each of the main parties: Telemachus, Penelope, and the Suitors in the presence of Odysseus; his final vision is a fitting prelude to the fatal shooting contest of the next book.

# CHAPTER VII

# THE SUITORS

In the first Book of the *Odyssey* Athene, disguised as Mentes, visits Telemachus, who is hard pressed by the Suitors of his mother Penelope. Athene advises him how to act. The following lines are a part of her advice: 'If you hear that he (*scil.* Odysseus) is dead and no longer living, then return to your own native land, and heap up a grave mound for him, and perform funeral rites, a great many as it is fitting, and give your mother in marriage to a husband. But when you have accomplished these things and brought them about, then consider in your mind and heart, how you may kill the Suitors in your house, by stealth, or openly.'[1] This suggestion by Athene has been criticized as futile and senseless, because the Suitors would of course—so it is assumed—leave the house of Odysseus after the wedding.[2] This assumption is based on the more fundamental one that the Suitors feast in the palace of Odysseus in order to press their suit for the hand of Penelope. Both these assumptions need testing.

In the public assembly of the second book Antinous certainly puts the blame for the evil situation of Telemachus on Penelope and her delaying her marriage. He suggests that she is concerned with her own fame, and so lets her son lose his property, and he concludes by saying that they will not go to work, nor anywhere else, until she has married of the Achaeans whomever she wishes.[3] After the omen of the two eagles,[4] Eurymachus expresses much the same attitude, but shot through with an ugly violence. He ends by saying that they will not go after any other woman but Penelope. Again, when Penelope in Book 18 upbraids the Suitors for their novel and objectionable mode of seeking a wife, Antinous promises gifts, but, repeating his own words of the Ithacan assembly, says that they will not go to work, nor anywhere else, until she has married of the Achaeans whomever she wishes.[5] This is what the leading Suitors, Antinous and Eurymachus, say in public, at the assembly of the people and in the great hall of Odysseus' palace when everybody is present; and the same is still upheld by Agelaus in Book 20, just before Athene deranges the mind of the Suitors, when he says to Telemachus: 'But you sit down beside your mother and tell her this, that she should marry whoever is the best man and offers most, in order that you may happily enjoy all your heritage, eating and drinking, and she may look after another man's house.'[6] This is what in fact Telemachus has done, as we know from Penelope.[7]

But when in Book 16 Antinous returns without having caught Telemachus, 'they themselves all together went into the place of assembly, and they let no-one else sit with them, neither young, nor old.'[8] This is then a private assembly, and we may expect to hear the Suitors' real view of the situation. The gist of Antinous' speech is this: 'Let us kill Telemachus. While he is alive, we shall not achieve these things; he will turn the people against us. Therefore let us kill him, divide his possessions between us and give the house to the mother's husband. But if you want him to live, and to have all that his father had, then let us not consume his possessions coming together here, but let each one woo Penelope from his own house seeking her with bridal gifts, and let her then marry whoever offers most and comes fated.' This speech shows unambiguously that the Suitors' presence in the house has little to do with their wooing of Penelope. If the only or even the main concern of the Suitors was to win Penelope, they would do so from their own homes. Their feasting in the house of Odysseus is directed against Telemachus, prospective heir of Odysseus' possessions, house and kingship. As early as in Book 1 Antinous cannot but show that he grudges Telemachus the kingship, and the hypocritical words of Eurymachus do nothing to veil this.[9] In the Ithacan assembly Leocritus indicates that even if Odysseus himself were to come home, the Suitors would not leave the palace, even though Penelope would of course no longer be available, but they would stay and kill Odysseus.[10] As the scales are turning against the Suitors, they can no longer veil their true minds. When Eurymachus fails to string the bow, he says that he is 'not so much grieved about the marriage', though it makes him sad—there are many other women available—but that they are so much inferior in strength to Odysseus that they cannot string his bow.[11] What matters most then to Eurymachus is power, not marriage with Penelope, and we understand here how much his earlier words of ardent admiration were worth.[12] Finally, Eurymachus states the true situation as far as Antinous is concerned, when Antinous has fallen by the first shot of Odysseus: 'He lies dead now who was the cause of it all, Antinous. For he set on foot these actions, not so much needing or wanting marriage, but having in mind another thing which the son of Cronos did not fulfil for him, that he should be king among the people of well-founded Ithaca himself and that he would kill your son from an ambush.'[13] It is plain that if at least in the earlier part of the epic the impression is produced that the Suitors are in the palace in order to woo Penelope, this impression is produced by the Suitors themselves intentionally.

But we may ask the question whether the poet intends us to be deceived, or whether he gives us the chance to realize the true situation in spite of the Suitors' efforts to hide it. In the first book Telemachus explains the situation in the house to Athene-Mentes. He concludes by saying that they are consuming his substance by feasting, and that they will soon smash him himself, words which he repeats when he gives the same explanation to the beggar Odysseus in Eumaeus' hut later.[14] It is plain from the very outset that the Suitors, by dwelling in the house of Odysseus, intend to diminish the wealth of Odysseus and Telemachus. Telemachus complains of it in the Ithacan assembly and to Menelaus in Sparta, and so does Eumaeus to the beggar Odysseus.[15] The tremendous wealth of Odysseus is proudly enumerated by the loyal herd.[16] But three years of daily feasting on the part of over a hundred guests would diminish even a wealth of that size. The possibility of the Suitors making an attempt on Telemachus' life is foreshadowed already in the young man's angered and apprehensive words in Book 1.[17] The Suitors play with the idea that he might not return from his journey, after the Ithacan assembly.[18] The plan to kill him is mooted by Antinous when he realizes that Telemachus has actually gone on his journey, and the Suitors are well aware that in planning to murder the son they, the Suitors of the mother, are playing a strange game.[19]

In the later part of the epic, the words of Penelope herself state the situation unambiguously. When she has heard of the Suitors' attempt on her son's life, she bitterly reproaches Antinous for ingratitude towards Odysseus: 'His substance you are now consuming and bringing to shame, you woo his wife, you try to kill his son, and me you greatly distress.'[20] When she appears to the Suitors in all her beauty in order to elicit gifts from them, she points out how different from time-honoured custom their manner of wooing is, how instead of bringing gifts into the house of the prospective bride they are consuming the substance of her house.[21] The veil of irony is very thin here. When Penelope institutes the shooting contest, she speaks the blunt truth about the Suitors' wooing: 'Listen to me, Suitors mannish beyond the limit, who have long been eager to devour this house and continually drink it to destruction, while the man of the house is away, for a long time, and you were not able to put forth any other story, but that you desired to marry me and take me to wife.'[22] It could not be said more plainly that the Suitors' intention in feasting in the palace of Odysseus is not to woo Penelope, but to destroy his wealth and with it his prestige.

In addition, Odysseus himself sums up the offences of the Suitors as 'shearing the wealth of the man and robbing his wife of honour', words which are repeated by Halitherses in the second Ithacan assembly.[23] On this view, the Suitors' wooing of Penelope is not only 'rather novel', as Penelope herself had ironically suggested, but it is a diminution of her honour, an insult.

Let us return to Athene's advice to Telemachus in the

first book. We know now that the Suitors desire the house and the treasure belonging to Odysseus, which is the basis of his kingship, even more than the hand of Penelope; and we also know that if Penelope married one of the Suitors, her new husband would take over Odysseus' palace and position, and Odysseus' treasure would be divided among all the Suitors. This means that, even after Penelope's remarriage, Telemachus would have to fight to the death for his own heritage. We must then conclude that Athene's injunction is perfectly reasonable, in fact very much to the point. But in order to see this we have to change our view of the *Odyssey*: it is not a fairy story of princes competing for the hand of a beautiful queen, but it is a tale from times in which power based on wealth and brute force was little hampered by law,[24] a tale of greedy and ambitious aristocrats trying under a thin veneer of courtliness to seize the absent king's wife, wealth and position.[25]

# CHAPTER VIII

# TELEMACHUS

It is well known that in the course of the *Odyssey* Telemachus grows from boyhood to manhood.[1]

In Book 1 the action is set in motion when Athene gives him 'might and courage',[2] and so releases him from the impotence in which he seemed fettered by the presence of the Suitors and the lack of his father. In his new-found power he immediately asserts himself: first against his mother, whom he sends upstairs, saying: 'Speech will be the business of men, all of them, but mostly myself. For mine is the power in the house'; and secondly against the Suitors, whom he addresses uncompromisingly as 'Suitors of my mother, men of overbearing violence and insolence.' In his naive spiritedness he tells them that he will call an assembly for the next morning and there in public order them to leave his house. When Antinous suspects the influence of Zeus behind young Telemachus' courage and shows his fear that Zeus might make him king, Telemachus speaks lightly of the possibility of becoming the supreme king of Ithaca and the islands, but again insists on his lordship in his father's house.[3]

Athene, leaving Telemachus, flies off like a bird: 'And he with his mind grasping this was amazed; for he believed that it was a god.' Asked by Eurymachus who the stranger was, Telemachus gives the name Mentes, the Taphian, and hides his recognition of the deathless goddess.[4] In fact, he deceives Eurymachus; he is beginning to acquire his father's wiliness.

In Book 2 he enters into the sphere of public action for

the first time, calling an assembly of the Achaeans and taking
his father's seat. He asks for removal of the Suitors from
his house and for a ship to go abroad, and is defeated on both
scores. But the evil-doing of the Suitors has been made
public, and Zeus has shown on whose side he is by sending
the omen of the two eagles; the eagle is of course the bird of
Zeus. The private plight of Telemachus has become a public
injustice which will be punished.[5]

After his defeat, Telemachus seeks solitude on the beach
and prays to Athene, putting his situation before her. She
comes in the guise of Mentor, encourages him again, and promises a ship, thus fulfilling what Leocritus had suggested in
the assembly without expecting it to be fulfilled, a fact which
is plain from the Suitors' later surprise at hearing of Telemachus' departure.[6] Telemachus is learning to trust in the
goodwill and power of the goddess.

Meeting Antinous, Telemachus refuses to return to his
former easy-going relationship; but he is now a fully grown
man, is finding out what the situation is, and his spirit within
him is increasing. This means that physically, intellectually,[7]
and in terms of spirit and courage, he feels adult. Therefore
he says: 'I shall try to hurl black death upon you.'[8] Here
the young man declares war on his enemies. His first step in
this direction is deceit: he says that he is going as a passenger
on someone else's ship, since he has not succeeded in obtain-
ing a ship and rowers himself. He also hides his departure
from Penelope, telling only Eurycleia about it and ordering
her to keep it from his mother for a while to save her anxiety.
When Telemachus orders his companions to bring the pro-
visions to the ship, the poet calls him for the first time 'Holy
power of Telemachus'.[9] He is now imbued with the strange
unaccountable power of a hero. But as he embarks, he is
still led by Mentor who is Athene; and she sits down first,
and then he close beside her. So they depart for Pylus.

Let us at this point take stock of the things that matter
to the poet in the growing up of Telemachus, and follow them
separately. Physically, Telemachus has reached the size of a
man. He has experienced the personal presence of Athene
with wonder and prays to her for help in need. Understanding

the situation fully, he has found the courage to challenge the Suitors. He has claimed the lordship of his father's house, and has toyed with the delight of being the supreme king of the realm.

The physical maturity of Telemachus is remarked on by others: the maid Eurynome speaks to Penelope of the young man growing a beard;[10] and for Penelope this becomes decisive for her decision to arrange for her remarriage.[11] The final proof that Telemachus has grown to the full physical power of a hero comes when he tries to string the bow of Odysseus, and at the fourth time would have succeeded if Odysseus had not given him a sign to desist.[12] In the battle with the Suitors he takes his full share; and in the closing book Laertes is delighted to see his son and his grandson vying with each other in valour.[13]

Although Telemachus has recognized Mentes as being a god or even Athene, and although his prayer to Athene is immediately granted,[14] he does not realize that Mentor is not his father's old friend. Supported by Mentor in his voyaging, helped by him over his painful shyness in facing Nestor, he does not believe that with the help of Athene he could deal with the Suitors, as Nestor suggests. He says: 'That would not happen to me though I were hoping for it, not even if the gods wanted it so.'[15] Athene, in the guise of Mentor, scolds him, saying: 'A god if he wishes can easily save a man even from afar.'[16] Telemachus changes the subject; he does not believe that the gods either would or even could help him out of his plight. When Mentor leaves, revealing himself as Athene by flying up in the form of a bird, the Achaeans and Nestor are amazed, and Nestor speaks of a great future for Telemachus. But we are told nothing about Telemachus himself. Athene does not accompany him to Sparta; he is sufficiently experienced now to travel on with a human companion, Pisistratus, son of Nestor. In the meeting with his father, Telemachus is granted an immediate demonstration of the power of the gods: the dirty old beggar suddenly appears as a splendid strong man. Telemachus believes that this is a god. When Odysseus tells him who he is Telemachus will not believe it: 'A mortal could not devise this by the strength of his own mind, unless a god came himself and, if he so wished, with ease made him young or old.'[17] He only believes when Odysseus explains that this is indeed the work of Athene 'who makes me such as she wishes—for she has the power— now a beggar, and now again like a young man dressed in fine clothes'. And Odysseus adds: 'It is easy for the gods, who have the broad heaven, to increase a mortal man splendidly or to worsen him.'[18] But in spite of this demonstration Telemachus is not yet ready to include faith in the succour of the gods in his planning for the future. For when Odysseus suggests that Athene, together with Father Zeus, might be sufficient helpers in the battle against the Suitors, Telemachus answers: 'Excellent indeed are the helpers that you mention, though they sit high up on the clouds; they do hold sway over men and the immortal gods.'[19] This reply is ironical, but only in part.[20] Telemachus no longer doubts the power of the gods to do what they want, as he did in the presence of Nestor and Athene. This is quite clear in his last sentence, even if his first sentence is tinged with irony. But what Telemachus still doubts is that the gods will actually come down from heaven when the battle is on. Odysseus, however, is certain that they will not stay away long in the crisis, and Telemachus is ready to follow him in the end. For when father and son make their plans and discuss whether to 'test' the maids in the house and the men on the farm, Telemachus is impatient to get into the fight: 'But let us see to this later, if indeed you know a sign (*teras*) from aegis-bearing Zeus.'[21] Odysseus does not at this point answer the question that is implied. But he later prays to Zeus for a sign from him, and Zeus thunders; and again, when Odysseus has strung the bow, Zeus thunders, and Odysseus is delighted that Zeus has sent a sign.[22] Telemachus is then well on the way to trusting in the help of the gods. Similarly, when Odysseus and Telemachus remove the armour from the hall and Athene lights up the place for them, Telemachus is amazed at the brightness everywhere and says: 'Surely a god is in the house, one of those who inhabit the broad sky.'[23] Odysseus replies: 'Be silent, and control your mind, and do not ask questions. This is the way of the gods who inhabit Olympus.' Odysseus curbs his son's curiosity. He is experienced in traffic with the gods and has both more faith and more reverence in relation to them than the younger man. But the poet makes it plain that this is something that the growing hero and prospective heir to the supreme kingship is learning under the guidance of his father.

The relationship of Telemachus to the Suitors is complex. In Books 1 and 2 discussed above, and in the battle at the end of the epic, it is a matter of straight enmity. In the rest of the poem the tension of power between the two parties is played out in terms of the institution of guest-friendship.[24] This becomes for Telemachus the testing ground for his manhood.

In Book 1 Telemachus does for Mentes, his guest, what he can. He welcomes him immediately and offers him a meal, well away from the Suitors so that he may not be annoyed by them. He explains the embarassing situation in a whisper, and only then—that is, after the meal—asks about Mentes' name and city.[25] He finally offers him a bath, entertainment and a gift.[26] All this takes place in a corner of the hall, out of the road of the Suitors who pursue their roisterous feasting as usual. The Suitors take no notice of the stranger until he is gone, so that the impotence of Telemachus to protect his guest does not become evident, although there are hints of it in his removing the stranger's seat to the side and in his caution in speaking to his guest. But here Telemachus fulfils the duties of hospitality promptly and courteously and as well as he can in a difficult situation.

In Books 3 and 4 Telemachus is himself the guest in the great royal houses of Pylus and Sparta. When, in the end, urged on by the words of Athene, he wants to leave Sparta in a hurry, even before daybreak, Pisistratus restrains him from cutting short the hospitable farewell that Menelaus is bound to offer him; and so Telemachus leaves with beautiful gifts from Menelaus and Helen and some good advice from Menelaus on the right measure in guest-friendship.[27]

The first test of Telemachus as 'host' confronts him as soon as he sets foot on his native island. Leaving Pylus, Telemachus had been asked by the fugitive seer Theoclymenus for a passage on his ship, and he had granted the request.[28] When they land in Ithaca, Theoclymenus asks Telemachus where he is to go, to someone else's house or to his.[29] Telemachus explains that under ordinary circumstances he would tell him to go to his own house. But since he was going to be away in the country, and Penelope stayed upstairs and would not see him, it would be of no advantage to him to go there. He suggests therefore that Theoclymenus should go to Eurymachus, 'whom the people of Ithaca now regard as equal to a god; for he is by far the best man, and he desires more strongly to marry my mother and to seize the (royal) honour of Odysseus'—if Zeus will let him. Here Telemachus refuses to offer hospitality to a man who asks for it and whom he has helped already. Instead he sends him to the man who is most powerful in Ithaca, and who has the best prospects of marrying Penelope and of becoming supreme king of Ithaca. This means that Telemachus assumes that Eurymachus will be the supreme king, and that he himself does not intend to make any attempt to claim his father's throne. But if Eurymachus is the most royal man in Ithaca, he will give the most generous hospitality to the stranger. So Telemachus intends the best for the stranger by his suggestion.[30] The immediate reply from the gods is an omen: a hawk carrying a dove, sent by Apollo. Theoclymenus interprets it: 'There is no family (*genos*) more royal than yours among the people of Ithaca, but you are the stronger always.'[31] This divine assurance changes the attitude of Telemachus completely. Delightedly he greets the seer as guest-friend, and asks a loyal companion to offer him hospitality until he himself returns home. Here, lack of confidence in his own powers and rank causes Telemachus to refuse hospitality to the seer until Apollo shows him what the standing of his family is. In this first test Telemachus would have failed without the help of the gods. The second test follows immediately. When Telemachus arrives at the hut of Eumaeus, Eumaeus hands over to him the stranger Odysseus who is a suppliant. Telemachus says in anguish: 'The words you have spoken pain my spirit. For how can I receive the stranger in my house? I myself am young, and do not yet trust my hands to ward off a man, when he first offers violence.'[32] Also, his mother is undecided whether to stay or go. He therefore suggests that Eumaeus should keep the stranger with him, and that he, Telemachus, will provide food and clothes. It is at this point that Odysseus himself, in the guise of the strange beggar, teaches his son, whom he must pretend not to know, a lesson in hospitality: 'If I had youth in addition to the spirit that is in me or if I were the son of noble Odysseus . . . , I should fight the Suitors, even if they were to kill me, rather than see strangers ill-treated in the house . . . "[33] Here the ill-treatment of strangers is mentioned as the first of the Suitors' shameful deeds; their seduction of the maid-servants and their endless feasting follow. What Odysseus here demands of his son is to fight the Suitors even at the risk of his life, because among other things they ill-treated the strangers in his house. Telemachus replies with an enumeration of the many Suitors, with reference to his mother's indecision, to the wasting of his substance and the danger to his own life. He concludes with the words: 'But this lies on the knees of the gods.' He still has not the confidence that he can protect a beggar in his house against ill-treatment by the Suitors.

But then the situation changes: the old beggar becomes Odysseus, and Telemachus is now no longer alone. On the other hand, his position as the host of his father, disguised as a beggar, among the Suitors is even more difficult. For Odysseus forbids him to use force in his defence; he may only 'command them to stop their folly, admonishing them with gentle words'. Apart from that, Telemachus must learn to control his heart when he sees his father suffering.[34] The only means then that Telemachus will have to defend his guest is the power of his words; and this guest is his father whose fate to some extent depends on his handling of this difficult situation.

As soon as Odysseus arrives in the palace, Telemachus gives meat to Eumaeus for the stranger with the message that he should go the rounds and beg.[35] When Antinous scolds Eumaeus for bringing the beggar, Telemachus prevents a quarrel. When Odysseus is struck by a stool from Antinous' hand, Odysseus himself replies, and the other Suitors side with him against Antinous and his excessive violence. In consequence, Telemachus does not need to interfere; he grieves greatly for his father, but sheds no tear, learning to control his heart.

In Book 18 Antinous overhears the quarrel between Irus and Odysseus and suggests that they should be made to fight each other for the prize of sausages, as an entertainment for the company. With this suggestion he seems to arrogate to himself a power which is not his.[36] But even though the Suitors at Odysseus' request swear that they will not attack Odysseus however Irus fares, Telemachus[37] assures the stranger that he is safe from any attack or interference. His justification is this: 'I am the host (lit. 'receiver of strangers') and the two kings approve, Antinous and Eurymachus, sensible both.' By these words Telemachus shrewdly guards his position as the one who is ultimately responsible for the stranger's well-being, over against Antinous who has instigated the duel.

When Penelope, stirred by Athene, shows herself to the Suitors, she upbraids Telemachus for his lack of sense in allowing the stranger to be ill-treated by the Suitors.[38] Telemachus, knowing that she is ignorant of who the beggar is, defends himself with great moderation.

The counterpiece to the initial scene between Antinous, Odysseus and Telemachus is the final scene of this book between Eurymachus, Odysseus and Telemachus. Eurymachus mocks Odysseus, who retaliates fiercely in words. Eurymachus, angered, hurls a foot-stool at him which misses him but fells a cupbearer. Telemachus[39] answers him frankly but with great moderation. He speaks his mind, but does not drive the Suitors from the house; for he is the host. Amphinomus brings the incident to an end on a less hostile note by saying: 'Let us leave the stranger in the house of Odysseus for Telemachus to look after; for to his friendly house did he come.' With these words, the poet picks up the claim that Telemachus made earlier: 'I am the host.'[40]

The next phase in the struggle for power, which again turns on the treatment of the stranger, follows at once, when in Book 20 Telemachus seats Odysseus and gives him food.[41] He warns the Suitors in no uncertain words not to molest the stranger with word or deed. The Suitors led by Antinous bite their lips in anger at his bold speech, but acquiesce for the moment. But when the meal has been prepared and everybody, including the beggar, has received his equal portion, then Ctesippus, a rich, lawless man, without any provocation, offends most drastically against the demands of hospitality: after ridiculing the stranger he throws at him an ox-foot as a 'guest-gift'. Odysseus avoids it, and it hits the wall. This challenge calls forth from Telemachus the strongest words he has yet spoken: he would have killed Ctesippus if the missile had struck the beggar. In a speech which expresses his awareness of being fully adult now and his utter disgust at the present situation, he concludes by saying that he would rather die than witness the Suitors' deeds any longer. The last three lines are an exact repetition of Odysseus' teaching when he first met his son in the swine-herd's hut, as yet an unrecognized beggar.[42] Telemachus has truly learned to be a 'host of strangers'; and that means, as we have seen, that he has now the mind of a king.[43]

In Book 21 comes the final test. Some of the Suitors have tried in vain to draw the bow, and Odysseus asks for permission to try it himself.[44] Antinous angrily rejects the request. Penelope intervenes, pointing out that it is 'not good nor just to treat improperly the guest-strangers of Telemachus whosoever comes to this house'.[45] She says that she will of course not marry the beggar, if he should succeed in drawing the bow; and in reply to Eurymachus she says that the Suitors need not be afraid of being shamed by the beggar; their good name is lost already through their behaviour in the house of Odysseus. But she promises ample gifts to the stranger if he draws the bow. At this point Telemachus asserts his supremacy: 'My mother, none of the Achaeans has greater power than I to give or refuse the bow to whomsoever I will, neither all those who rule in rugged Ithaca, nor those on the islands towards horse-feeding Elis. None of them will force me against my will even if I want to give this bow to a stranger to take away with him for good.' He then tells his mother to withdraw to her rooms and that 'his is the power of the house'.[46] He has said this before, but at that time his power was concerned with the bard's song.[47] Now what is at stake is

his protecting the stranger by fulfilling his request; and this
means that what is at stake is whether the mighty weapon,
the bow, will be given into the hands of Odysseus or not.
Odysseus' safe return to his kingdom rests in his son's hand.
The decisive moment comes when the swineherd has carried
the bow halfway across the hall, but, frightened by the angry
shouts and threats of the Suitors, stops and lays it down. Then
Telemachus turns in anger against him and threatens to chase
him with stones into the country: 'I am stronger than you.'
And he passionately wishes that he could send the Suitors
home also! This fierce outburst turns the Suitors' mood from
wrath to laughter, and Eumaeus safely takes the bow to
Odysseus.

Telemachus has finally learned to face the Suitors on behalf
of the guest-stranger; and it is this that places Odysseus in
the position to deal with the Suitors. This is the climax in the
development of Telemachus and the dramatic turning-point in
the plot.

The consummation of it all is reached in the final scene of
the epic.[48] When Odysseus and his company go out for the
last fight, Odysseus asks Telemachus to show himself worthy
of his forefathers, and the young man answers: 'You will see,
dear father, that in this spirit of mine I do not shame your
race, as you say.' Old Laertes is delighted and says: : 'What a
day this is for me, dear gods! I am very glad; my son and my
grandson vie with each other in valour!' When Laertes has
killed Eupithes, Odysseus and Telemachus proceed to the
attack together.

# CHAPTER IX

# ODYSSEUS

The character of the 'man' whom the poet glorifies in the *Odyssey* is in the main shaped by the values of the society to which he belongs. The supreme excellence or *arete* in the *Iliad* is the strength and skill of a warrior and his prowess.[1] But, besides this, praise is given to the capacity to give counsel and to speak well.

In the *Odyssey*, intelligence and cleverness take the first place, though in a hero they must necessarily be combined with strength, skill and valour. Telemachus becomes prudent and wise as he awakens from childhood. He says to Penelope in self-defence: 'But I in my heart grasp and know each thing, both what is good and what is not so good. But previously I was foolish.'[2] He is often called wise or shrewd (*pepnymenos*). Penelope has 'an excellent mind and knows how to look to her own advantage', and 'she knows thoughts such as the great heroines of the past did not'. So Antinous says about her.[3] Athene, the goddess, is herself 'renowned among all the gods for her intelligence and cleverness in seeking her own advantage.[4] When therefore Athene says of Odysseus, 'You are the most excellent of all mortals in counsel and words',[5] he is not alone in this *arete,* but he is supreme among men.

The image of Odysseus' strength and skill is his great bow.[6] It needs sheer physical power to string the bow, and strength coupled with skill to shoot through the axes in the contest of the Suitors. The decisive part played by the bow at the end of the poem is foreshadowed throughout. In Book 1 Athene disguised as Mentes mentions the poison that Odysseus procured for his arrows.[7] Among the Phaeacians whom he has defeated in discus throwing Odysseus says: 'I know how to handle a well-fashioned bow. I should be the first to strike a man with my arrow in the midst of the foe, even if my companions stood close by and shot with arrows.'[8] Among his contemporaries only Philoctetes was his superior in archery; but he would not wish to vie with the great archers of the past, such as Heracles, or Eurytus who had to pay with his life for challenging Apollo to a contest. Odysseus meets Heracles, the mighty archer, in the Underworld: 'He was like dark night, his bow bared and an arrow on the bowstring, glaring about terribly, for ever like one who is just going to shoot.'[9] Heracles compares the toils of Odysseus, especially his journey to the Underworld, with his own labours when he says: 'Unfortunate man, in truth you too experience an evil destiny, just as I bore under the rays of the sun.' The poet here presents Odysseus and Heracles as a pair in fate: the two who went to Hades alive, the two great archers. It is through Odysseus' bow that Penelope decides to select her new husband among the Suitors at the end of her meeting with the beggar Odysseus in Book 19.[10] Before this meeting, Odysseus and Telemachus with Athene lighting the way have removed all the armour from the hall. It is essential at this point that *all* the armour should be removed; Telemachus has the sword and spear which he has on him, but Odysseus has nothing but his bare hands and no means of getting his own great bow—the one long-range weapon of many arrows which is kept carefully locked up— until Penelope makes her decision. The scene of the removal of the armour at the beginning of the book prepares for and balances Penelope's decision to bring out the bow at the end of the book.[11]

The great bow is at the centre of Book 21. Its importance is built up carefully at the beginning. As Penelope goes to fetch it, its history is told in detail: it used to belong to Eurytus, the great archer who vied with Apollo.[12] Iphitus, the son of Eurytus, gave it to Odysseus as a guest-gift. The bow's importance is further enhanced by the description of the mighty door which Penelope has to open to enter into the

innermost chamber where the bow hangs on a nail. The
opening door roars like a bull grazing in the meadow. The
simile underlines the weight and size of the door. This simile
is balanced by a pair of similes at the end of the book illuminating the climax of the contest which is the theme of the
whole book: Odysseus stringing the bow is compared with a
bard putting a string round a new peg on his lyre; and when
he plucks the taut string, it sings beautifully, 'like unto a
swallow in voice'.[13]

In the battle with the Suitors the decisive weapon is of
course the bow. There is even a short critical span of time
when Odysseus has nothing and nobody to protect him from
the Suitors but his bow.[14] When in the last book the ghost
of Amphimedon recounts the killing of the Suitors, he mentions no other weapon but the bow of Odysseus.[15]

The supreme intelligence and craftiness of Odysseus is
acknowledged by Zeus himself; it is praised by Nestor; and
when Odysseus introduces himself to the Phaeacians, he refers
to his wily tricks as that for which he is known among men
and famous as far as the heavens.[16] It is apparent in his
invention of the Wooden Horse, in the ample fiction of his
lying tales, in the clever trick of blinding the Cyclops and
hanging on to the bellies of the sheep, and so on.

It is often contrasted with *bie,* sheer brute force. This is
most explicit in the Cyclops episode. When Odysseus from his
ship shouts back to the Cyclops that it was Odysseus, city-
destroyer, son of Laertes who blinded him, the Cyclops
remembers an ancient oracle foretelling this. But he always
expected that Odysseus would be a big and handsome man,
clad in great battle-might, but now he was little and a mere
nothing and without strength, though he overwhelmed him
by wine.[17] When Odysseus recalls this incident to his com-
rades, he puts the contrast even more precisely: 'the Cyclops
cooped us up in the hollow cave by his mighty force, but even
from there we escaped by my excellence, counsel and mind.'[18]

But in the *Odyssey* as we have it, the intelligence of Odysseus
is much more than cleverness and inventiveness, although this
as such is obviously much appreciated by a Greek audience at
any time. It is primarily practical reason of great power

capable of controlling spontaneous impulse and even strong emotion, both in others and in the hero himself. It is this side of Odysseus' character that I want to study in detail.

It is described for the first time by Menelaus.[19] Odysseus, Menelaus, Diomedes, Anticlus and other Achaeans were sitting inside the Wooden Horse on the citadel of Troy when Helen came, and by imitating the voices of their wives tried to entice the heroes whom she suspected of being in the Horse to betray themselves. Both Menelaus and Diomedes desired either to rush out or answer from within. But Odysseus kept them back; and he controlled Anticlus, who would not be persuaded, by clasping his hand over his mouth until the danger was passed. Menelaus calls Odysseus *talasiphron*, 'endurance-minded'. His cleverness in inventing the Wooden Horse would not have conquered Troy if he had not also had the power to counter Helen's wiles by controlling the impulsive actions of his friends.

In the cave of the Cyclops everything depends on Odysseus controlling his own impulse. When the Cyclops has eaten two of Odysseus' companions and lies asleep stretched out between his sheep, Odysseus plans to kill him with his sword; but then another spirit held him back.[20] For they would all have perished, since none but the Cyclops could shift the mighty rock which closed the entrance of the cave. Again the first reaction, if followed, would have been fatal, but Odysseus counters it within himself.

This process of gaining control over a first impulse that might lead to disaster is most fully described at the beginning of Book 20, when Odysseus lying abed in the porch sees his disloyal maid-servants coming out of the hall to join their lovers, the Suitors. 'Then his spirit was roused in his breast', and he considered whether he should leap after them and kill them one and all, or let them go once more, for the last time, 'and his heart barked within him, like a bitch who standing over her helpless puppies barks at a man whom she has not recognized as a friend, and wants to fight, thus his heart barked within him indignant as he was at their evil deeds.'[21] Odysseus' feelings towards his own household and all those who belong to it are as intense and fierce as those of a bitch for her young, and the disloyal maids are like a stranger to the dog; they have forfeited their place in the household. But Odysseus restrains himself: 'Striking his chest he scolded his heart: "Endure now, my heart! You have endured worse on the day when the terrible Cyclops ate our strong companions. But you endured until intelligence led you out of the cave though you thought you would die." Thus he spoke, addressing with urgency his own dear heart in his breast.' Here the effort of Odysseus to gain control over his anger is represented in the form of a dialogue between him and his heart. He reminds his passionate heart of an earlier occasion when the heart's readiness to endure was rewarded by his clever mind finding a way out. The heart's response is described in an image: 'And to him his heart remained in bonds enduring unceasingly.'[22] Here Odysseus' control over his passion is expressed by the image of a 'bond' or 'fetter' with which his heart is tied. The bonds with which Odysseus is tied to his ship's mast when he passes the Sirens act in the same way; when his heart wanted to hear their song, and he indicated to his companions that they should loose him, they tied him down with more bonds, as he himself had commanded.[23]

This same quality of Odysseus is described most explicitly by Athene when she first meets him again in Ithaca.[24] The scene is a recognition scene, but a peculiar one. For in it Odysseus tries to avoid recognition, but is of course known to Athene; and Ithaca, hidden in mist by Athene, is recognized by Odysseus, step by step, the two motifs moving in counterpoint, as it were. As Athene wraps the island in mist, Odysseus believes that it is once again a strange place fraught with danger, and wails in dismay. Athene, disguised as a young noble shepherd, approaches, and Odysseus asks what this land is. The young noble describes it, and finally names it as Ithaca. Odysseus is delighted, but hides his identity under a fictitious tale, as he will do again and again in the second half of the epic and to good purpose. But here this is ineffective and indeed humorous, because the other person is not human, but a goddess. Athene, much amused, reveals herself, and Odysseus stands recognized. With a smile she describes his character, which is so pleasing to her: his capacity to obtain his advantage, his stealth, the variety and inexhaustible force of his inventive mind, his capacity to deceive, his command of thievish words, in short his excellence 'in counsel and words', a description which is called forth and proved true by his fictitious tale. Then she turns to the immediate situation and tells him that he must endure of necessity, and divulge to no one, man or woman, that he has come back from his wanderings, but must suffer in silence much pain, putting up with the violence of the Suitors. What Athene commands and foretells here is the fierce self-control that Odysseus will have to exercise in the face of the Suitors' insolence. But Odysseus is not yet ready to consider future action. He is peeved and reproachful towards the goddess, and does not trust her. He believes that she may be mocking him, and that she wants to deceive him about this land being Ithaca. This caution and fear of being deceived, which is evident on many occasions,[25] calls forth another appreciative description of his character from Athene. It is this capacity to distrust and hold back, even when all his heart's desire would drive him towards believing, that Athene praises in striking words.

She calls him *epetes, anchinoos* and *echephron*.[26] Unfortunately the meaning of *epetes* is quite uncertain. The meaning 'courteous'[27] does not fit the context, because the preceding speech of Odysseus is, if not rude, certainly not courteous. The meaning 'eloquent' from *eipon* or *epos*, which has also been suggested, fits precisely, because Athene's praise of Odysseus is then concerned with both the quality of his mind or thought and his eloquent speech in this passage as in her previous appraisal of his excellence 'in counsel and in words'.[28] *Anchinoos* occurs only here. *Anchi* expresses a relationship of mutual closeness; the word *anchitheos,* for instance, means 'close to the gods' or 'having the gods close'. Correspondingly, *anchinoos* means 'having one's mind close to oneself'.[29] Just as in Book 20 Odysseus keeps his barking heart in bonds, so he is here said to have his mind close to himself, ready to use it. With a different image we should call this 'presence of mind'.[30] Thirdly, Athene calls Odysseus *echephron*. Apart from this passage, the word is used seven times of Penelope.[31] It is probably more specific than 'having good sense', though this is possible. Hephaestus, deceived by Ares and Aphrodite, shouts to Zeus that his daughter is beautiful, but not *echethymos*: she does not keep in check or control her high-spiritedness or desire.[32] Taken on this pattern *echephron* describes a person who is in control of his or her mind and feelings.

Athene supports her characterization of Odysseus by describing his attitude to meeting Penelope and Telemachus: 'Another man coming home from his wanderings would heartily desire to see in his house his children and his wife; but to you it is not yet welcome to learn and find out, not until you still test your wife.'[33] Here Odysseus is contrasted with a more ordinary sort of man who on returning would immediately want to see his loved ones, but Odysseus has the self-possession to proceed with much more circumspection. Before talking to his wife in order to 'learn and find out'[34] how they have all fared during his absence, he wants to test Penelope. This takes place in Book 19, to which we shall turn presently.

Finally, Athene responds to Odysseus' urgent wish to know for certain whether this land really is Ithaca: she points out landmarks and lifts the mist. He is at last convinced and kisses the life-giving earth of his homeland in his great joy.

In this scene Odysseus comes to recognize his own land, Ithaca; and in the process the poet, through the words of Athene, tells us explicitly what manner of man Odysseus is, in preparation for what is to follow. Everything will depend on his power to keep a firm hold on himself whether he is provoked by the hostility of the Suitors or assailed by pity for his wife.[35] When we turn to the first meeting between Penelope and the beggar Odysseus in Book 19, we know through Athene's words in Book 13 that this will be a scene of 'testing'.[36]

After the Suitors have gone,[37] and when Odysseus and Telemachus have removed the weapons from the hall,[38] Odysseus says to Telemachus: 'But you go to bed, and I shall remain here so that I may still provoke the maids and your mother; and she, wailing, will ask me questions about everything.'³⁹ Odysseus' intention is to provoke the maids and Penelope. We have seen already that provocation may form part of the theme of testing.⁴⁰ What precisely is the purpose of such provocation? Odysseus' companions try to prevent Odysseus from provoking the Cyclops, the 'wild man'.⁴¹ But he does, and the Cyclops prays to Poseidon to harm Odysseus and then hurls a rock at the ship for the second time. The provocation causes violent action.⁴² Chryses, priest of Apollo, comes in order to ransom his daughter, captive maid of Agamemnon. Agamemnon sends him rudely away: 'Go, do not provoke me so that you may return home in safety.'⁴³ A provocation may lead to violence.⁴⁴ When the seer Theoclymenus has left, 'the Suitors all looking at each other tried to provoke Telemachus, laughing at his guests.'⁴⁵ In the speech that follows the insolent young men mock Telemachus for his bad luck with his guest-friends: a useless beggar and now a prophet. But Telemachus 'did not heed their words, but silently looked at his father', waiting for him to attack the Suitors. Here the Suitors try to provoke Telemachus into an outburst of passion, but he controls himself and waits. But his anger is evident. Provocation causes anger.⁴⁶ When Menelaus has won the duel with Paris, Zeus 'tried to provoke Hera with mocking words'⁴⁷ by the suggestion that Menelaus might now go home with Helen and that Troy might be left to stand. Athene, Hera's close companion in this situation, is seized by fierce anger, but she is too afraid of Zeus to speak. But Hera could not contain her anger in her breast, and she spoke. Her speech makes Zeus angry. Here provocation causes anger and quarrelling. In Book 5 Athene wants to get her own back on Zeus. She tries 'to provoke him with mocking words': 'Father Zeus, will you be angry with me for what I am going to say?'⁴⁸ But he, 'father of men and of gods' that he is, smiles, and is not to be roused. Here Athene would certainly like to provoke him into anger.

All these contexts show that *erethizo* denotes 'provoking' with the intention of causing anger expressing itself in violent words or actions. The attitude of the 'provoker' may be fiercely hostile or more mildly hostile, but it is certainly devoid of affection or sympathy. This—we must conclude for the time being—is Odysseus' attitude when he intends to 'provoke' the maids and Penelope.

The plan to discover the attitude of the maids and the men of the household had been mooted by Odysseus in Eumaeus' hut: 'But let us alone, you and myself, get to know the attitude of the women, and we might also test someone among the menservants to see who honours and fears us in his heart, and who does not care and dishonours you, though you are a man.'[49] Telemachus replies that it would take too long to test each man. But he suggests they should get to know the women who dishonour their master and those who are free of guilt.

Odysseus first encounters the maids when, after nightfall while the Suitors are still present, they come in to light up the hall.[50] The beggar proposes that he will see to the lighting, and that they should go upstairs and work in the company of the queen. This does not suit the maids, who want to be with the Suitors. Melantho, who makes love to Eurymachus although she owes her upbringing to Penelope, inveighs violently against him, telling him to get out of the hall. The beggar replies with a threat, referring to Telemachus, and the maids flee in terror.

It is this scene that Odysseus refers to when he says that he will 'still' provoke the maids.[51] The Suitors have left now, but the beggar is still in the hall when the maids return to clear up. The very presence of the beggar is a provocation to Melantho who attacks him fiercely, threatening to strike him with a burning torch. Odysseus answers gravely and warns her of what might happen to her, referring again to Telemachus. At this point Penelope intervenes and firmly silences Melantho. Provoked by Odysseus, Melantho has certainly responded with angry hostility and threats of violence: her disloyalty is plain. The poet picks up the theme of the disloyal maids once again at the opening of Book 20, a scene which we have described above.[52] They suffer their just, if cruel, death after the battle with the Suitors.[53]

When Odysseus warns Melantho he at the same time provokes Penelope when he says: 'I fear that your mistress may be angry with you and rage against you.'[54] Penelope rises to the challenge and rebukes her firmly; she is doing her duty by her husband and his household in controlling the maids and protecting the stranger.

Penelope begins the conversation with the beggar by asking who he is. Addressing the queen in reply for the first time, Odysseus uses a word which means both 'woman' or 'lady', and 'wife', expressing in this way immediately nearness and distance, the keynote of this scene.[55] Then he praises her glory in the most exalted imagery. Her 'fame reaches the broad sky, like that of some noble king who, godfearing, ruling over many powerful men, upholds just ways, and the black earth bears wheat and barley, and the trees are laden with fruit, and the sheep bear young without fail, and the sea provides fish, owing to his good leadership, and the people prosper under his rule.' Odysseus, himself such a king,[56] could not give her higher praise than to draw this picture of a godly and just king's realm in which everything, crops, fruit, beasts, fish and men, prosper together.[57] But is this praise justified? Odysseus goes on to say that 'therefore' he is ready to answer questions on other things, but not about his family and homeland, because there is too much grief connected with the memory of it. He says 'therefore' because he is contrasting his misery with the blessed prosperity of the queen; it would be ill-fitting to tell her of such misery. Further it would not be right to sit groaning in a strange house 'since it is rather a bad thing to grieve indiscriminately for ever'.[58] He might become a nuisance. Now, if Odysseus intends to provoke Penelope to anger and perhaps violent words, what is he doing in this speech towards that purpose? Her answer makes it plain: she emphatically and flatly rejects this praise.[59] All her excellence and her beauty have been destroyed by the gods, since the Greeks, and with them Odysseus, went to Troy. Her glory depends on his presence and care. Then she draws the true picture of Ithaca, her realm as it really is, and it is the complete opposite of the just king's realm.[60] The nobles of the islands and of Ithaca itself woo her against her will, and they consume her household. That is violence and injustice with impoverishment as the consequence. She herself therefore from grief is neglecting her duties; she does not care for the strangers, the suppliants, or the heralds. But she has resisted the wooing of the Suitors by weaving and undoing the shroud of Laertes which is now, by compulsion, finished: she can no longer find a way out to escape another marriage.[61] The picture that she draws of her own situation and the state of her household with all the people, beasts and possessions that belong to it could not be bleaker. By his praise of the blessedness of justice Odysseus has provoked Penelope into telling him the true state of affairs and her own true mind. Penelope does tell the strange beggar all this, not because she trusts him, but because he has provoked her.[62] When Odysseus speaks of the pain that the thought of his family and homeland causes to him, this is true: he means Ithaca and his, that is Odysseus' family of course, and the contrast between a just king's realm and Ithaca is as bitter to him as it is to Penelope when she speaks about it, but she is of course ignorant of these overtones. But when the beggar will not 'grieve indiscriminately for ever', she seems to feel this as a reproach and a challenge: she acknowledges, as we have seen, that she is neglecting some of her duties from grief. But the detailed account of the trick of the weaving is self-justification: she kept the Suitors at bay. Odysseus has indeed 'provoked' Penelope; and under the pressure of his testing she has given him full information about the situation in the palace and about her own attitude to it.

When Penelope asks the beggar once again who he is, he is ready to answer. He pretends to be a grandson of the Cretan king Minos, a son of Deucalion, and brother of Idomeneus who was a beloved and respected guest-friend of Odysseus. In the beggar's tale Odysseus arrives storm-driven in Crete after Idomeneus has left for Troy, and he is entertained with generous hospitality by Idomeneus' brother, the beggar. The concrete detailed description brings the image of Odysseus very close to Penelope so that she bursts into tears. The intensity and abundance of her weeping is pictured in the simile of snow melting and rivers in spate.

Here Odysseus, by vividly calling up the memory of Odysseus, has provoked Penelope, not to anger and violence, but certainly to a passionate outburst of grief. While in the first 'round' Odysseus provoked Penelope into stating the situation and showing her mind on it all, he now provokes her into showing her heart by her abandoned grief.

But the very effectiveness of his test of Penelope becomes a danger to Odysseus himself. As she wept for her husband—who was sitting beside her—'Odysseus in his spirit pitied his mourning wife, but his eyes stood as if of horn or iron without trembling between his eyelids; and from guile he kept back his tears.'[63] Here the tension and opposition is between the 'spirit' of the man that is filled with pity, and his 'guile' which causes him to control his emotion. The outward expression of this control is the steady gaze of his eyes, their unyielding hardness being pictured by the comparison with horn and iron.[64]

The power of mind which makes this control possible is Odysseus' greatest quality: his *dolos*. When *dolos* denotes a quality of mind, and not a trap or trick, Cunliffe translates it by 'guile, craft, cunning, trickery'. These words are misleading, because for us they imply moral disapproval, if not condemnation. It is plain that our passage implies no such negative judgement; on the contrary, the very fact that in Book 13 Athene praises Odysseus for wanting to test Penelope indicates that all that Odysseus does in testing Penelope is admirable and splendid. We must therefore ask how 'guile' in general, and particularly as here practised in relation to one much beloved, can be part or even the crown of a man's excellence.[65]

What the best things are in life, in the eyes of Odysseus, for a woman is apparent in his wishes for Nausicaa: 'May the gods give you all you desire in your heart, a husband and a household, and may they grant harmony of mind, a noble thing; for there is nothing stronger and better than when a man and a woman in oneness of mind control a household; much pain to their enemies and much joy to those who wish them well; and great fame do they themselves gain from it.'[66] What matters for our question is that, if in the Homeric world the life of a man and a woman at the head of a house is at its best, it is a bane to their enemies and a joy to their friends.[67] This opposition between friends and enemies is stated as something simple and obvious and ever present. The ground for it is the social structure of Homeric society.[68] The basic social unit is the *oikos,* the household at the head of which is the noble warrior with his wife, together with his sons and unmarried daughters and sons' wives, perhaps also with his parents. Further members of this household are the retainers and slaves, both in the palace and on the farms belonging to it. The *oikos* also consists in the palace itself, the lands, farmsteadings, and all the animals owned by the noble; and finally much of the glory of the *oikos* consists in the treasure of gold, silver, bronze and so on, amassed as booty or by piracy or as guest-gifts. Such a household forms a close-knit independent unit which may at any time be hostile to another such household.

We have already seen that *dolos* is often contrasted with *bie,* 'physical force'.[69] In the Homeric world these are the two means by which a man can fight whether in aggression or defence. The tribe of the Cyclopes gathering round the cave of the blinded roaring Cyclops ask: 'Surely no one is killing you by guile or by force?'[70] And the Cyclops replies: 'No one is killing me by guile, but not by force.' Athene refers to the same alternative when she advises Telemachus to consider how he can kill the Suitors 'either by guile or openly'.[71] 'Openly' here means of course by open violence as contrasted with the hidden stealth of guile. In Homeric thought both 'force' and 'guile' are a hero's glory if he can wield them; and he will use them to the bane of his enemies and to the joy and comfort of his friends. Value judgements are here limited by the interests of the warrior and his 'household', and only occasionally by the wider unit of the 'city' (*polis*) or even the Achaeans over against the Trojans.

If *dolos* on the other hand is used by a stranger or enemy, the hero, who is intelligent and capable of guile himself, is cautious and distrustful: he is aware that he might be caught in a 'trap'. So Odysseus distrusts Leucothea and her veil, and also Circe, and Athene in our passage.[72]

It is only when *dolos,* or *bie* for that matter, are allied with injustice that they are judged to be evil. The violence of the Suitors is evil for this reason;[73] and there is no glory in the 'trap' (*dolos*) that Clytemnestra sets for Agamemnon: the bard's song about her will be odious among men, and she will give a reputation hard to bear to women, even one who acts well.[74]

To turn to Odysseus, before Troy and during his wanderings guile in conjunction with physical power is his equipment as a man fighting against the Trojans on behalf of the Greeks, and against anyone hostile, for the sake of his own survival. When he comes home, the situation is little different. His household is invaded by enemies who, for all Odysseus knows, may have won over most of the members of his household to their side. It is for this reason that Odysseus, coming in disguise, tests everyone in the household for their loyalty—except Telemachus, his own son, whose loyalty he does not doubt, although he realizes his weakness. Such testing (Type 1) of necessity implies guile. As against a possible enemy Odysseus has to cover up his identity by lying tales; and his words have to be such as to provoke the other person into betraying his or her real mind.

Why does Odysseus approach his own wife Penelope like a potential enemy and traitor? The background to this is what happened to Agamemnon at the hands of Clytemnestra. In the Underworld Agamemnon has warned Odysseus not to be gentle towards his wife, and not to tell her all that is in his mind;[75] and in his planning with Athene Odysseus expresses horror that his fate might have been the same as Agamemnon's.[76] It is true then that Penelope might be her husband's deadliest enemy, and that is what Odysseus has grasped. This is why Odysseus provokes and tests her, and why, when pity for her grief threatens to overwhelm him, he restrains his tears with guile. He succeeds because he is master of his own heart, as he was in the Wooden Horse, and as he will be in relation to the traitorous maidservants.[77]

Only when the Suitors are dead and all possible risk of Penelope in any way causing difficulty is excluded, does the poet represent Odysseus once as being provoked into an outburst of passion. This is when Penelope tests him regarding their marriage bed.[78] But there is also no longer any need for holding back.

To sum up, our interpretation of the meeting of Odysseus and Penelope in Book 19 up to the point to which we have taken it[79] bears out the description of the hero given by Athene in Book 13.[80] He is indeed 'master of words', *epetes*, if that is what the word means; he forms a compact unity with his own intelligence, and he is in control of his heart. The testing scene in Book 19 brings out with particular force Odysseus' capacity to endure, not only external hardships, but the impact of his own feelings without deviating from the path indicated by his guileful intelligence which leads him to test his wife without revealing himself to her.

Even at this early stage in the development of Greek thought we meet the opposition of the heart or desire or passion with intelligence or guile. Odysseus, in controlling the first and following the lead of the second, foreshadows, within his own epoch and culture, Plato's good man whose soul is directed by reason.

# CHAPTER X

# PENELOPE

Penelope is the main female figure in the *Odyssey*. She is a heroine, one of the great women. Antinous, leader of the Suitors, compares her with Tyro who, loved by Poseidon, bore Neleus father of Nestor, with Alcmene who, loved by Zeus, bore 'bold-spirited lion-hearted Heracles', and with Mycene, ancestress of the famous city of much gold and centre of power in the Mycenaean Age.[1] Antinous even goes so far as to say that in force of intelligence and insight Penelope excels them all.

Penelope is also of heroic stature physically. She is a big woman.[2] When she goes to fetch the bow of Odysseus, she takes the bronze key in her 'stout hand', just as Odysseus with a 'stout hand' breaks off a branch to cover his nakedness.[3] When Athene wants Penelope to impress the Suitors, she makes her ''bigger and stouter to look at', just as she makes Odysseus 'bigger to look at and stouter' when he is to encounter Nausicaa, or to be recognized by his wife.[4]

Penelope is devastatingly beautiful when she shows herself to the Suitors, her veil drawn to her cheeks, flanked by a servant-maid on either side.[5] The knees of the Suitors are loosed, and their hearts are bewitched by desire, and they all pray that they might lie beside her in bed.[6] Eurymachus praises her as excelling all women by the beauty of her figure, her size and the mind that is 'even within her'. Finally they all bring the most precious gifts. Penelope in her beauty has indeed, as Athene intended, 'spread out'[7] the Suitors' hearts so that they are no longer firmly knit, but loose and flabby, no longer intelligent and purposeful, but inane and stupid. Penelope makes effective use of her beauty in order to gain treasure for the house of Odysseus.[8]

The 'great excellence' of Penelope is praised by the spirit of Agamemnon in the second Underworld scene: 'How good the heart and mind were of noble Penelope, daughter of Icarius! How well she remembered Odysseus, her wedded husband!'[9] The word translated by 'heart and mind' is *phrenes* which is an organ capable of both thinking and feeling;[10] the word 'good' means both 'virtuous' and 'capable'. This is

the picture of a woman who out of her 'good sense' is utterly loyal and obedient to her husband, and uses her intelligence and guile to hold fast to him under terrible pressures.

## Penelope Weaving

Antinous acknowledges Penelope's intelligence and cunning in the Ithacan assembly.[11] He explains that for three years, and now into the fourth, she has been deceiving the Suitors by sending messages and secret promises to each of them separately. 'And she has thought out in her heart the following trick in addition':[12] she began to weave a great garment to be a shroud for Laertes, and she asked them to wait with hastening on her marriage until she had finished it. For three years she undid at night what she wove in the day. In the fourth year she was found out, and was compelled to finish it.

This is the position at the beginning of the action of the *Odyssey*. Over three years have passed in which the situation was more or less stationary: the Suitors feasting in the palace, the boy Telemachus oppressed and sad, Penelope upstairs weaving the shroud of Laertes. Now, as the weaving has come to an end, the Suitors will become more urgent, and Penelope will have to act.[13]

In Homeric thought 'weaving' implies more than making a garment. What a person weaves (grammatically speaking, the object of the verb 'to weave') is of course often a cloth or a garment. But it may also be a 'plan', 'trick' or 'counsel'. The Suitors were weaving their 'plan' to kill Telemachus, when the herald Medon overheard them.[14] Penelope wants to let

Laertes know in case he might weave a 'way out' of a difficult situation.[15] Athene says to Odysseus that she has come to weave a 'plan' with him, and he asks her to weave a 'plan' so that he may wreak vengeance on the Suitors.[16] In each case the devising of the plan needs resourcefulness, intelligence and cunning. When the sea nymph Leucothea tells Odysseus to entrust himself to her head veil and to let go of the raft, he is afraid that one of the immortals may be weaving a 'trick' against him.[17] Caught in the cave of the blinded Polyphemus Odysseus 'sought to weave all tricks and a plan, since it was a matter of life and death'.[18] In the *Iliad*, an ambush laid against Bellerophon is a 'trick' that the king weaves; and in the council of the Achaeans, they 'wove words and counsels for them all'.[19] There is then a close association between the activity of weaving and the devising of a clever plan or even deceitful trickery.

To return to Penelope, Homer has chosen to represent her as weaving a great garment for Laertes for three whole years and more; and this image of the queen weaving and, of course, also undoing the garment is called up three times, by Antinous, by Penelope herself, and by the ghost Amphimedon.[20] Through it Penelope is characterized as exceedingly skilful, intelligent and resourceful, in fact, as 'cunning' in both its senses.[21] Antinous, after telling the story of her weaving, is compelled to acknowledge this, however angry he is to have been duped by her. He says that Athene has given her 'to  understand very beautiful works, and a good mind, and to know gain'.[22] The 'beautiful works' are the clothes she weaves. What a treasure such a garment woven by a queen's hand could be is apparent from the parting gift of Helen to Telemachus: a garment 'which was most beautiful with embroidery and the biggest and shone like a star'.[23] Penelope's 'good mind' and her understanding of 'gain' are precisely pictured when she weaves, since weaving, as we have shown, is so closely associated with intelligence and cunning.

Penelope, sitting upstairs weaving at her loom while downstairs in the hall the Suitors feast for three years without  pestering her, is a masterly representation of the intellectual power of this woman who by her cunning succeeds in keeping over a hundred Suitors at bay. They enjoy their feasting, of course; and they are thereby decreasing the wealth of Odysseus and Telemachus, which is their intention. But apart from that, they are duped by Penelope.

The story of the 'weaving' of Penelope has then a double function in the *Odyssey*. First, it takes the action of the epic to the point where Penelope's remarriage can no longer be avoided; and secondly, it shows the superior skill and intelligence of the queen.

## Penelope's Decision to Arrange the Bow Contest

The greatest proof of Penelope's loyalty to Odysseus is, however paradoxical it sounds, her decision to arrange the bow contest among the Suitors for the purpose of selecting her new husband. That she comes to this decision in the course of a conversation with her husband whom she does not recognize is a masterpiece of poetic invention and a source of rich dramatic irony.

The presupposition is of course that Penelope does *not* recognize Odysseus, in fact has no inkling that the beggar might be Odysseus. The poet has made it quite clear earlier that such is his intention. When Athene spreads mist round the sleeping Odysseus after his arrival in Ithaca, she does so 'to give herself time to make him unrecognizable and tell him the circumstances in order that his wife should not recognize him, nor the townsmen and friends, until the Suitors had paid for all their transgression.'[24] Talking to Odysseus, Athene tells him that he must not divulge to anyone of the men or women, any of them, that he has come back from his wanderings.[25] When Odysseus makes his plans with Telemachus he says: 'No one shall know that Odysseus is in the house. Neither then shall Laertes know, nor the swineherd, nor any of those belonging to the house, nor Penelope herself.'[26] Actually the only three people who apart from Telemachus get to know of Odysseus' presence are Eurycleia who recognizes him accidentally, and the two herdsmen, Eumaeus and Philoetius. They are told by Odysseus himself at the last possible moment, because their help is needed for the battle with the Suitors. The only time that mention is made of

Penelope conspiring with Odysseus in instituting the bow contest is at the end of the poem, in a speech of the dead Suitor Amphimedon in the Underworld. We shall return to this presently.[28]

Penelope's decision in Book 19 is carefully prepared for.  In Book 18 Penelope appears before the Suitors, and for the first time before Odysseus who is among them as a beggar. This is preceded by a short scene which sets things in motion and introduces the main themes. It is Athene who stirs in Penelope the desire to show herself to the Suitors. Athene's purpose is that Penelope should 'spread out the spirit of the Suitors',[29] and that she should become more highly prized by her husband and her son than before.[30] When Penelope expresses her intention of appearing before the Suitors and of warning Telemachus against them to the old maidservant Eurynome, this woman suggests that she should wash and anoint herself, since it is bad to grieve endlessly. 'For,' she says, 'your son is now of such an age, whom you fervently implored the immortal gods to see growing a beard'.[31] However difficult this sentence is, it clearly means that Penelope had been praying for the time to come when Telemachus would grow a beard, that is, attain to manhood, and that that time had now come. But Penelope is not willing to be festive, for her beauty has disappeared with Odysseus' departure for Troy. But while she waits for the two maids to come who will accompany her, Athene pours sweet sleep over her and makes her exquisitely beautiful. Penelope, awaking, wishes that Artemis would send her death as gentle as that sleep so that she might no longer have to mourn for Odysseus.

The important points in this scene are: the effect that Penelope's appearance is to have on the Suitors, and her husband and son; the news that Telemachus has begun to grow a beard, and that this matters a great deal to Penelope; and finally the old news that Penelope is sad to death at the loss of her husband.

The effect of Penelope's beauty on the Suitors is instantaneous: 'Their knees were loosed, they were bewitched by desire in their spirits, and they all wanted to lie in bed with her.'[32] Then she, who had been amazed at her son's masterful words in Book 1, and spoke of him as 'still a child with little knowledge of the toils of life or speaking in the assembly' in Book 4,[33] acknowledges publicly before the Suitors that he is 'big' now, and has 'reached the measure of young manhood'.[34] She upbraids him for allowing the fight between the beggar Odysseus and Irus. He accepts her acknowledgement of his manhood, and replies to her reproach with modesty, adding a curse against the Suitors. Next Eurymachus addresses Penelope, praising her incomparable beauty. She rejects his praise of her excellence and her beauty which, as she says, the Immortals destroyed when Odysseus went to Troy; great and noble would certainly her life be if he came home and cared for her. But as it is she is full of grief. She goes on to tell Eurymachus—and with him all the Suitors—what Odysseus said to her when he departed for Troy. After entrusting her with the care of his household, and especially his father and mother, he said: 'But when you see our son growing a beard, then marry whomever you want, leaving your house.'[35] She continues: 'Thus he spoke; and that is now all coming about. There will be a night when the hateful marriage will come to meet me, accursed woman, whose happiness Zeus has taken away.' The time is then ripe for Penelope's decision. Telemachus is a man having grown a beard; it is now that, according to Odysseus' parting words, Penelope must marry another man. But she is still not ready to set a day for the wedding or make a choice among the Suitors, but instead she sidetracks the issue by eliciting presents. Odysseus is delighted because, by coming to meet the Suitors halfway, she extracts treasure from them which will enhance the glory of Odysseus' house. With the words 'she bewitched their spirit with her words, but her mind desired other things'[36] the poet describes Penelope's duplicity; for she seems to encourage the Suitors, but her real mind is very different;[37] and Odysseus knows this, because she has arranged to meet the beggar this very night to hear what he can tell her about Odysseus,[38] even though his own parting words are putting pressure on her not to delay remarriage indefinitely. The facts that will inevitably lead soon to Penelope deciding on marrying one of the Suitors are clearly represented in Book 18.

In Book 19 Penelope meets Odysseus disguised as a beggar, and is provoked by him, as we have seen,[39] into showing her own view of the situation and her feelings at the memory of Odysseus as he was when leaving for Troy. She rejects the exalted praise of the beggar with the same words as the lustful praise of Eurymachus.[40] But after that, under the lash of the beggar's provocation and in the freedom of speaking to an outsider, she says much more than she would ever say to any of the Suitors. Having described the situation in the house, she acknowledges her own remissness in caring for strangers, suppliants and heralds out of grievous longing for Odysseus.[41] On the other hand, she has spent her time in evasive tricks, in particular in weaving and undoing the shroud of Laertes. But now she has been compelled to finish it. She continues: 'Now I can neither escape marriage nor can I yet find any other trick. But my parents very much urge me to marry, and my son chafes at their devouring his substance, knowing it full well. For now he is a man fully capable of looking after his house and a man to whom Zeus gives glory.'[42] Here Penelope states clearly and explicitly the reasons for having to marry again: the shroud is finished, and Telemachus is a man; marry she must, as Odysseus had said. But she is not yet ready to decide when and whom she is going to marry. Instead she changes the subject and asks for the second time about the beggar's descent. When, after the beggar's tale of giving hospitality to Odysseus before he went to Troy, she has wept her fill, she takes the initiative with a new thrust of energy: she 'tests' the beggar to see whether he has really entertained her husband in his house, and asks him about Odysseus' clothes, his own appearance and about his companions.[43] The beggar describes Odysseus' brooch, his clothes, and his personal herald in detail. Penelope recognizes the 'signs' as authentic, and weeps for joy.[44] Through the proof of the signs her relationship to the beggar is changed. She says to him: 'Now, stranger, though you roused my compassion before, you will be a friend in my house and held in honour'.[45] On the other hand, because this recognition of Odysseus refers to the time before the Trojan War, there is no cause for hope for Penelope, and she says: 'I shall not receive him coming back to his own country'.[46] Then Odysseus tries to soothe her grief. He tells her how quite recently among the Thesprotians he heard of Odysseus' impending return, that his treasures were lying deposited in the house of King Pheidon while he had gone to Dodona to consult the oracle whether he should return openly or hidden[47]—a choice piece of irony, as this is told by the 'hidden' Odysseus. The beggar goes on to foretell under oath that Odysseus will come at the New Moon. In this speech, which is half truth, half fiction, and which is designed to bring the thought of Odysseus close and to praise him, particularly for his successful pursuit of treasure,[48] Odysseus intends to test Penelope's reaction to the possibility of Odysseus returning almost immediately. The theme of testing is here most abundantly ornamented; for this is still its second phase: for the third time Odysseus tries out Penelope's reaction, in this case to Odysseus' immediate coming, which is the key question, and the only one asked by Odysseus in the simple form of testing applied to the swineherd and the goatherd.[49]

Penelope might well have gained some hope through this prophecy. There had been other events that pointed to Odysseus' coming and punishing the Suitors. When Telemachus returns from his journey, Penelope is eager for news.[50] She is told what Menelaus learned from Proteus, namely that Odysseus is kept prisoner by Calypso; and the seer Theoclymenus prophesies that Odysseus is coming or is already present in Ithaca. Penelope expresses the wish that it might come true, and promises to the seer her friendship and gifts if it does. That is all—in her eyes the story about Calypso presumably matters little, because it does not speak of Odysseus' return; and the prophecy is to her nothing but the unproven word of a stranger. When the beggar Odysseus arrives at the palace and encounters the violence of the Suitors, Penelope sends Eumaeus to call him to her.[51] Speaking to Eumaeus she wishes fervently that Odysseus might come home who together with his son would exact vengeance for the violence of the Suitors. As she speaks, Telemachus downstairs in the hall sneezes mightily. Penelope laughs with delight at the good omen, and sends Eumaeus to call the

beggar. For now, she says, none of the Suitors will escape
from death; and she promises a reward to the beggar, if she
finds him speaking the truth. But her hopefulness is short
lived. In Book 18, awakening from the gentle beauty sleep
that Athene has sent to her, Penelope wishes that Artemis
might send her, even at that moment, death as gentle as that
sleep so that she might no longer have to consume herself
with longing for her husband.[52] In Book 19 Penelope only
wishes that the beggar's prophecy might come true, and
promises much if it does. 'But,' she says, 'in my heart, I think
as in fact it will turn out to be: Odysseus will not come home
any more, nor will you be sent to your destination'.[53] Penelope
rejects the hope that is held out to her. There are no signs
here to guarantee the authenticity of the beggar's words.

But while she has no hope regarding Odysseus, she has
been roused from her apathy of grief. She will no longer neg-
lect strangers.[54] The beggar has been proved by signs to have
been a host to Odysseus, so now Penelope will offer him hospitality to the best of her ability, in Odysseus' absence; her
fame depends on it.[55] But because Penelope does not know
that the beggar is Odysseus, her energetic action becomes dangerous for him. She orders her maids to wash him, and make
him a comfortable bed, and to look after him in the morning.
She insists that none of the Suitors shall annoy him after this.
The 'foot-washing' which Penelope offers to the beggar is then
an expression of her guest-friendship. Odysseus refuses a
comfortable bed, and will allow his feet to be washed only by
an old woman who has suffered as much as he himself.[56]
Eurycleia, a little later, understands very well what he means
when she says that he will not let the younger women wash his
feet in order to avoid their jeering and insolence.[57] Penelope
tells Eurycleia to wash her Master's age-mate, and she says
thoughtfully that Odysseus' hands and feet must be rather
like those of the beggar. Eurycleia weeps, and addresses the
absent Odysseus with love and sorrow, and compares his
probable sufferings from insolent maids with the sufferings
of the beggar in front of her. Turning to him, ready to wash
his feet, she says that she never saw a stranger as much like
Odysseus as him; and the beggar agrees that this similarity

has been remarked on by others. At every step we move nearer to a recognition. Odysseus, suddenly remembering his scar, quickly turns towards the darkness.[58] But Eurycleia, touching the scar, recognizes him at once—it is done: Penelope will also recognize him by the scar; and the two will make a plot to kill the Suitors. There follows a long story about how Odysseus got the scar, in the form of a full appositional expansion.[59] After it, the poet returns to the recognition of Odysseus by Eurycleia,[60] and describes in full how she dropped his foot, and spilled the water, how with tears of joy she addressed him, and looked towards Penelope to tell her, but Athene turned her mind away,[61] and then Odysseus forced Eurycleia to promise not to breathe a word about his presence. This time it is revealed that there is a 'sign' which proves Odysseus' identity, but Athene and Odysseus combine to prevent it being revealed to Penelope. All through the long history of the scar, the audience probably expected comfortably that Penelope would share the recognition, and that a conspiracy between her and Odysseus would follow. When this does not happen, it has the charm of surprise, and the expectation of the 'recognition' continues. The danger for Odysseus is past.

Having fulfilled the requirements of guest-friendship, Penelope once more speaks to the beggar, though it is getting late. But he is now a dear and honoured guest-friend, no longer a pitiable stranger. Grief-torn like the nightingale, she wonders whether to stay beside her son or to marry the best of the Achaeans. As at the end of her first speech in this scene,[62] she comes round to the thought, and states it in full, that Telemachus when a child did not want her to leave the house, but now that he is a man he begs her to leave, because the Suitors devour his substance.[63] Penelope is on the point of making her decision. But once again she breaks off, because there is one more straw of hope. She tells the beggar about the dream she saw of her geese being killed by an eagle who revealed himself as Odysseus. The beggar Odysseus agrees with the message of the dream, that the death of the Suitors is close. But once again Odysseus' attempt to test Penelope's reaction to his immediate coming is frustrated by her unbelief. For once again Penelope rejects hope: this dream has come out of the ivory gate; and does not come true. There are then no good reasons for hope: the beggar's 'signs' referred to the time before Troy; his prophecy of Odysseus' return is unsupported by a 'sign', the 'sign' of the scar not being revealed to Penelope; and the dream, being a dream, may be false. In consequence, Penelope draws the conclusion she must draw, in obedience to Odysseus' parting words, now that Telemachus has grown to be a man: she decides on the bow contest as the means of selecting her new husband.

The beggar Odysseus urges her on, realizing that this will give him the chance to kill the Suitors; and once more he prophesies Odysseus' return before a decision will be made through the bow contest. Penelope replies with great courtesy, and indicates that it is time to go to bed.

Penelope's incredulity in this scene is foreshadowed earlier in the epic by Telemachus and by Eumacus. In Book 1 Telemachus tells Athene, disguised as Mentes, that his father has perished by an evil fate, and that it is no consolation to them if someone comes and says that he will return, since Odysseus' day of homecoming is lost.[64] Eumaeus tells the beggar that Odysseus has perished.[65] He says that no one coming and announcing Odysseus' return would be likely to persuade his wife and his son, and he describes how many a man, in need of help, comes to the palace, and ingratiates himself with the lady of the house by telling deceitful tales, and she weeps, and grants him hospitality.[66] Eumaeus suggests that the beggar might not act any differently, but Odysseus is dead. Beggar Odysseus swears an oath saying that Odysseus will come home.[67] But Eumaeus does not believe it.[68] Even after the beggar's long tale of his wanderings and hearing news of Odysseus who would come home soon, Eumaeus remains unpersuaded.[69] He no longer shares the wish of all others in the palace to hear the stranger's tales. For he has once been deceived by an Aetolian, and has waited in vain.[70] Here Odysseus replies: 'In truth you have in your breast an unbelieving heart! Not even by swearing an oath could I persuade you!'[71] Much later Eumaeus is persuaded by the 'sign' of the scar which Odysseus shows to him.[72]

The pattern of this scene between Eumaeus and Odysseus foreshadows the scene between Penelope and Odysseus with precision: the stranger's tale, and the unbelief. Eumaeus has believed once, was deceived, and since then will not believe. But Penelope has not been deceived, because she will not believe unless there are signs.[73]

After the killing of the Suitors, Eurycleia hurries up to Penelope's bedroom, and wakens her with the great news.[74] To begin with, Penelope refuses to believe anything at all. When at last she believes that the Suitors are dead, she still suggests that one of the gods killed them, because they deserved it. 'But Odysseus lost his homecoming far from Greece, and perished himself!' Then Eurycleia replies reproachfully: 'Your heart is for ever unbelieving,' and she tells her about 'a manifest sign', Odysseus' scar, how she recognized it, but was prevented by Odysseus from telling her. This moves Penelope to go and see the 'dead Suitors, and him who killed them'. Taking her seat opposite Odysseus, she is not certain of his identity, and wonders whether to test him.[75] Telemachus scolds her, saying that her heart is always harder than stone. But she will be persuaded only by the hidden 'signs' known only to Odysseus and herself. Once more, and for the last time, the 'recognition' is postponed. In a brief interlude,[76] Odysseus commands music and dancing in order to cover up the Suitors' death by the festive noises of what outsiders would suppose to be the queen's wedding. But the change to music and dancing is more than a realistic cunning dodge on Odysseus' part: it is also the poet's way of changing mood and atmosphere from battle and slaughter to the happiness of Odysseus and Penelope at last reunited. It is for this purpose also that Odysseus takes a bath, dresses in fresh clothes—he had previously spoken of his dirty and tattered appearance as a reason for Penelope's refusal to recognize him[77]—and is beautified by Athene. Then, taking his seat opposite Penelope, he taunts her with her stubborn heart which the Immortals have given her, which is indeed a heart of iron. In order to provoke her he asks the old woman to make up a bed for himself alone. Penelope in reply, 'testing' Odysseus, tells the woman to place it outside her bedroom.

Provoked to a burst of anger, Odysseus[78] replies that his bed cannot be moved, because part of it is an olive stump rooted in the ground. This is the 'sign' that Odysseus has for Penelope, a 'sign' which is also a beautiful symbol of the deep-rootedness of their mutual loyalty. Penelope recognizes the 'sign', and at last runs to Odysseus to embrace and kiss him. She asks his forgiveness for being so slow to recognize and welcome him, and she gives him her reasons: she was always afraid that someone might come and deceive her with his words, as so many men plan evil which is to their own advantage.[79] This is how Helen received infatuation into her heart by the will of a god, and from it sprang great evil, the Trojan War. Penelope concludes by saying that, since Odysseus has shown her the 'sign' of the bed, he persuades her heart, however stubborn it is.[80]

Penelope's unbelief is, then, a consistent feature of her character. The Greek word for this is her frequent epithet *echephron,* 'having good sense' or 'controlling her mind and feelings'.[81] Like Odysseus, she masters her impulses and proceeds with realism and caution. Penelope is certainly much in need of this quality in order to protect herself and her loyalty to Odysseus; and she is a worthy partner for him in her exercise of it.[82] On the other hand, her caution makes his attempt to test her in the end ineffective. It is her very loyalty that keeps Penelope at a distance from Odysseus until his identity is unmistakably proved.

To sum up, Penelope's decision in Book 19 to arrange for the bow contest is clearly motivated by Odysseus' parting words and by Telemachus having grown to manhood. Omens, prophecies and dreams make the coming of Odysseus as the avenger more and more imminent for the poet's audience; but they cannot divert Penelope from making her decision, because they are not proved authentic by 'signs'. It is then her utter loyalty to Odysseus and his 'will' that leads Penelope to decide on the bow contest, and to make this decision when she does.[83] The irony that she decides to proceed to marry another at the very moment when her beloved husband has returned and is beside her, and the fact that this decision, made in ignorance of his presence, will produce the bow which he needs for his battle, these things belong to the essence of Homer's craft.

The most striking so-called 'discrepancy' concerning Penelope's decision about the bow contest is found in the speech of the ghostly Suitor Amphimedon in the Underworld, who, in reply to Agamemnon's questions, recounts recent events in Ithaca.[84] Amphimedon says that Odysseus in his great shrewdness commanded his wife to arrange the bow contest for the Suitors.[85] Stanford and van Leeuwen before him maintain that Amphimedon here 'made a natural but incorrect surmise'. Kirk waves this aside as 'not a likely explanation of the inconsistency'.[86] It can however be shown, I believe, that this explanation is right and that Homer has a purpose in introducing this 'inconsistency'.

First of all, Homer makes it emphatically clear that the Suitors are not in the palace when Penelope talks to Odysseus. In Book 17 Penelope sends Eumaeus to the beggar to call him to her.[87] But he, in order to avoid the Suitors, who are prone to illtreat him, postpones coming until the evening. At the end of Book 18 the Suitors go home. In Book 19 Penelope and the beggar meet. The Suitors could not have known, therefore, how Penelope came to announce the bow contest. Amphimedon infers what is the simplest explanation. For, as Stanford says,[88] 'Few would have credited Odysseus with the super-human restraint of not making himself known to his wife till after his revenge.' But it is of course Odysseus' greatest excellence that he is able to control his feelings even under great strain.[89]

To support this sort of interpretation, we must see whether there are in the *Odyssey* other inconsistencies which are intentional. In Book 1 Athene-Mentes tells Telemachus that his father is still alive, but that cruel wild men are keeping him a prisoner.[90] But we have been told twice before that it is the nymph Calypso who keeps him back, first by the poet directly, secondly by Athene herself.[91] Athene-Mentes tactfully avoids mentioning Calypso to Telemachus, because he might become doubtful about his father's loyalty to his mother. The effect of the 'inconsistency' is graciousness and humour.

When Alcinous says to Odysseus that Nausicaa acted wrongly when she did not bring him with her to the palace, Odysseus replies that she had told him to come with her and her maids, but that he himself did not want to, from fear of the king's anger.[92] This is however not what actually happened. Nausicaa, embarrassed by the probability of gossip among the townsfolk, had asked him to stay behind at a definite place, and follow on somewhat later.[93] The discrepancy between Odysseus' account and what actually happened is clearly intentional: Odysseus lies tactfully in order to save Nausicaa from her father's anger. Homer expects us to realize and enjoy this when we hear Odysseus' words. In these two passages one of the characters in the epic produces the inconsistency for a particular reason.

When the Suitors hear Penelope uttering a ritual cry upstairs, they surmise that this is part of her preparations for the wedding that she will soon celebrate with one of them, while she is unwitting of the fact that the Suitors are out to kill her son.[94] From the Suitors' point of view this surmise is quite natural, but it is incorrect. We know that Penelope has uttered this cry after praying to Athene that she might save Telemachus from the murderous intentions of the Suitors. Here the wrong inference of the Suitors makes patent their simple-minded stupidity and callousness. The discrepancy is realized by the audience only, as in the case of the bow contest.

If the discrepancy between Amphimedon's account about the bow contest in Book 24 and the actual events in Book 19 is intentional, Homer must have had a reason for it. Stanford, speaking about 'recognition' in the *Odyssey*,[95] says that Greek audiences 'loved to be in the superior position of knowing a secret still unknown to participants in the story.' If Amphimedon had known exactly what happened, and simply retold the events, his story would have little interest. But as he infers rightly about the conspiracy of Odysseus and Telemachus, but wrongly, though with a naive plausibility, about a working together of Odysseus and Penelope, the audience even at this late stage in the story knows more than the participants in the action. For they know that Odysseus had much more shrewdness than to take the risk of involving Penelope in his fight against the Suitors; and they know that Penelope not only remembered her husband well for twenty years, but that she also remembered his parting words commanding her to marry again when Telemachus had grown up. However much she disliked another marriage, in obedience to his will she set up the bow contest in order to select her new husband, and by it provided her beloved husband with the weapon he needed. In this way, both Odysseus and Penelope are greater than either Amphimedon or Agamemnon know; but the audience knows, and enjoys the dramatic irony of the situation. If the story, as told by Amphimedon, is an older, well known version, and the much subtler turn of the story in Book 19 is Homer's own, the 'inconsistency' becomes even more piquant. In the older version there was no room for the exquisite elaboration of 'testing' and 'recognition', as we see it developed in Books 19 and 23 of Homer's *Odyssey*.

In conclusion, it is interesting to note how the two meetings between Odysseus and Penelope in Books 19 and 23 are built on the themes of 'testing' and 'guest-friendship'. Book 19 consists in Odysseus testing Penelope who in return tests his statement about having given hospitality to Odysseus. This leads to an act of hospitality on her part which almost leads to recognition. Under the pressure of Odysseus testing her, Penelope unfolds her situation and comes in the end to her decision. In Book 23 Penelope tests Odysseus successfully regarding his identity, and this finally brings about their reunion. Seen against the simple patterns of the underlying themes, the abundant and subtle ornamentation becomes all the clearer and more exquisite.

## Penelope's Position and Powers

The part which Penelope plays in the *Odyssey* has been a puzzle to many modern scholars. For within the clearly patriarchal society of this epic she seems to have the power to decide who is to be king in Ithaca by choosing a husband. Finley says that the Suitors 'placed the decision in the strangest place imaginable, in the hands of a woman', and that the 'prerogative' of bestowing rule in Ithaca 'mysteriously belonged to Penelope'.[96] He believes that the muddle is very ancient, and may rest on a 'confused vestige of mother-right system'.[97]

Let us begin by considering Penelope's relationship to the three men that are closest to her: her son Telemachus, her father Icarius, and her husband Odysseus.

In Book 1 Telemachus asserts his new-found authority as master of the house by telling Penelope not to interfere with the singer, but to attend to her woman's business; and she quietly obeys.[98] In Book 2 it is clear that Telemachus has the power to send Penelope back to her father's house.[99] But he has good reasons for not doing so: he would have to pay a large sum to Icarius, and he would be pursued by his mother's curse. In Book 21 Telemachus makes it plain that he himself, not Penelope, has the power to decide what is to be done with the bow of Odysseus.[100] He tells her again to attend to her own work; and again she obeys.

As far as Icarius is concerned, it appears from the words of Antinous that, if Penelope returned to her father's house, she would be obliged to marry whomever he commanded her to marry and who was pleasing to herself.[101] But even while Penelope stays in the house of Odysseus, her father and her brothers can exert strong pressure on her concerning the choice of her new husband. Athene urges Telemachus in a dream to hasten back to Ithaca: 'For already her father and brothers command her to marry Eurymachus.'[102]

Penelope's relationship to Odysseus is clearest from his parting words, and all that is connected with them.[103] We have already seen how the timing of Penelope's decision is determined by these words of Odysseus. But there is more. He says first of all: 'Let all things here be your care. Be mindful of my father and my mother in the house, as now, or still more, when I am away.' Odysseus' mother has died, and Laertes has retired to the country in his grief for his lost son. But 'all things here' are still to be cared for, and Penelope has accepted the charge which Odysseus has placed into her hands. In speaking to the beggar about her dilemma she wonders whether she is to stay beside her son and keep everything safe, her possessions, her servants and the lofty big house.[104] This means that the mastership of the house (*oikos*) is in Penelope's hands by Odysseus' decree until such time as Telemachus is old enough to take it over. Odysseus has also on leaving entrusted his friend Mentor with the care of the whole house, and asked him to obey the word of old Laertes, and to keep everything safe.[105] Mentor does try to defend the cause of Odysseus in the Ithacan assembly, but without much effect.[106]

The upshot of all this is that Penelope acts just as a mother, daughter and wife is bound to act in a patriarchal society. Through her obedience to the parting words of Odysseus, she has the power in the house, until Telemachus is ready to take it over. We have seen how Penelope, through her ruse of 'weaving' Laertes' shroud, has managed to remain in charge of the house for the last three years, in spite of over a hundred Suitors feasting in the hall every day. We have seen how she tries to fulfil the duties of guest-friendship as far as she can, even if at times her grief causes her to withdraw completely.[107] In Book 18 she makes use of the impact of her beauty on the Suitors to elicit gifts from them which will increase the treasure in the house of Odysseus.[108] In all these ways she cares for Odysseus' house, servants, and possessions as best she can.

So far there is no word about the kingship; and when Odysseus in the Underworld asks his mother Anticleia about the state of affairs in Ithaca, he asks two separate questions: [109] one about Laertes and Telemachus, whether they still hold the kingship (*geras*) or whether someone else has it; and the second one about Penelope, whether she is still with Telemachus and keeps everything safe or whether she has remarried. Here, the kingship and the power in the house of Odysseus are separate matters. The same is true when in Book 1 Telemachus demands the lordship in his father's house for himself, but is quite easy about the kingship; and this clear distinction between the two spheres of power is confirmed by Eurymachus' answer.[110] So far we have found no connection between Penelope and the kingship; her power is limited to the household of Odysseus.

Returning once again to the parting words of Odysseus, we learn that he told Penelope to marry whomever she wished.

With these words Odysseus placed the choice of her new husband into her own hands, not her father's, nor those of Telemachus, but her own.

At this point it is essential to realize that all modern notions about marriage, such as individual preference, love for a particular person, and so on, are irrelevant. That sort of choice was not open to a high-born woman like Penelope in such a society; and the possibility of such a choice is never mentioned anywhere. Penelope's choice is directed by the values of the society to which she belongs and which she shares. In talking to the beggar about the dilemma of her situation she describes her husband-to-be as 'the best (*aristos*) of the Achaeans who woos me in the house, and who provides countless bride gifts'.[111] There are two things that are important about Penelope's future husband: his *arete* and his wealth. But according to the form of the statement, his *arete* will be decisive. Other people mention the same two items. Antinous speaks of the man 'who provides most and comes fated';[112] and according to Athene, Eurymachus is backed in his suit by Penelope's father and brothers, because 'he excels all Suitors by his presents, and he is increasing his bride gifts'.[113] Both Telemachus and the Suitor Agelaus mention *arete* and gifts side by side.[114] Both Antinous and Odysseus speak of *arete* alone.[115] It is clear from these passages that when Penelope says she will marry the 'best man' who also offers much, she acts as she is expected to act within the structure of her society.

Jaeger says that *arete* 'denotes the strength and skill of a warrior or athlete, and above all his heroic valour. But such valour is not considered as a moral quality distinct from strength, in the modern sense; it is always closely bound up with physical power'.[116] The question for Penelope is therefore how to find the *aristos* among the Suitors. Her solution is the institution of the bow contest, a solution which fits firmly into its context in many respects. The life of the Homeric warrior consisted in competing with others for the first place, both in war and in peace.[117] The Suitors competed in sport while they were not feasting.[118] The fact that over a hundred of them wooed Penelope implies competition.[119] When therefore

Penelope institutes the contest of the bow she simply gives outward form to what is inherent in the situation.

But more than that: the choice of the great bow of Odysseus as the means of finding her new husband is the choice of her heart to the extent that feeling was allowed any place in the context. Whichever Suitor could string and use the bow of Odysseus was like Odysseus at least in that respect. Also, he would be worthy of the prize of the contest, Penelope herself. Telemachus opens the contest by saying: 'Begin then, Suitors, since this prize is set before you, a woman, such as there is no other now in the land of the Achaeans, neither in holy Pylus, or Argos, or Mycenae, nor in Ithaca itself or on the black mainland'.[120] Antinous even in anger had to acknowledge the greatness of Penelope;[121] and Eurymachus said that they, the Suitors, were vying with each other for Penelope, and no other woman, because of her *arete*.[122] The importance of the bow for Odysseus himself has already been described.[123] At this point it need only be pointed out that through his bow Odysseus becomes the measure of the man who will become Penelope's husband. Even up to this point, the kingship plays no part.

But there are three passages in which the marriage of Penelope and the kingship are mentioned together. First, when Telemachus does not feel equal to offering Theoclymenus guest-friendship in his own house, he suggests that he might go to 'Eurymachus, splendid son of clever Polybus, whom the people of Ithaca now look upon as they look upon a god. For he is certainly the best man, and desires most to marry my mother and have the kingly honour of Odysseus'.[124] Here Telemachus reports apparently on Eurymachus' wishes which are marriage with Penelope and kingship in Ithaca. As we have seen, however,[125] the omen of the hawk which follows means that the kingship will remain with the lineage of Odysseus, so that by the will of the gods the new husband of Penelope is debarred from the kingship.

Secondly, we have seen[126] that Eurymachus wants both Penelope and the kingship of Odysseus. Failing to string the bow, he grieves less about the loss of Penelope than about his inferiority in physical strength. Antinous wants the kingship more than the hand of Penelope. In entering into the contest of the bow, Eurymachus and Antinous therefore intend to compete for supremacy in physical strength, because this supremacy is going to ensure for one of them marriage with Penelope, and, what is more important to them, the kingship in Ithaca.

The relationship between superior physical strength and kingship has been discussed by Finley.[127] Homeric kingship was hereditary, as Antinous acknowledges,[128] if the heir was strong enough to defend his succession. If he was not, a stronger noble might scize the kingship. If Antinous—or Eurymachus—had won the bow contest, and thus shown his superior strength, he would have married Penelope certainly, but he would also have seized the kingship. As Telemachus, however, since his return from abroad, had shown increasing powers, and had almost strung the bow,[129] the Suitors realized that he might back his hereditary claim to the throne by physical force. In consequence, the noble who would usurp the kingship would have to do away with Telemachus. Plainly then it is the Suitors who turn the bow contest into a contest not only for Penelope's hand, but also for the throne of Ithaca.

Penelope herself, however, in her loyalty to Odysseus wants a man for her husband who is as nearly like Odysseus as possible, and so she makes Odysseus' bow the means of decision. There is nothing anywhere to suggest that Penelope expects to choose the new king by choosing a new husband. She expects to marry the *aristos* when she has found him, and to follow him to his own house, leaving regretfully the house of Odysseus,[130] as he had told her to do.[131] Furthermore, it is even absurd to assume that Penelope would choose a new king. For, as we have seen, Telemachus' claim to his father's throne was strong enough to force any other man who desired the kingship to deal with Telemachus by open fight or ambush. This is surely not the kind of situation that Penelope could be assumed to bring about willingly. For her the bow contest is the means of deciding about her husband, and nothing more.

Penelope does not possess any 'prerogative to bestow rule

in Ithaca'. On the other hand, when she chooses for her husband the man who is most valorous and also very wealthy, this man would certainly be in the best position to seize the kingship, if he wanted to, particularly if he added the house of Odysseus to his own possessions, as the Suitors had planned.[132] It is then the configuration of values in Homeric society and the Suitors' *hybris* which links the kingship in Ithaca with Penelope's choice of a husband, but not any power residing either in the person or in the position of Penelope: the most valorous noble who is also very wealthy is Penelope's choice; the same man is also most able to carry off the kingship.

# CHAPTER XI

# LAERTES

Laertes, father of Odysseus, does not appear in person until the last book of the *Odyssey*, but we are told about him by others. Athene, disguised as Mentes, speaks of the old hero who in his great grief lives away from the city on a farm and is cared for by an old servant woman who gives him food and drink when weariness seizes him as he slowly walks about in the vineyard.[1] But he still has at least some power if he will use it. For Odysseus, leaving for Troy, told Mentor 'to obey the old man (that is, Laertes) and to keep everything safe'.[2] Also, Penelope proposes to send a message to Laertes for advice when she fears for Telemachus' life.[3] In the Underworld, Anticleia describes to Odysseus Laertes' life on the farm: in the winter he sleeps with the slaves in the dust beside the fire, in the summer on piled-up leaves anywhere in the vineyard. 'There he lies grieving, and he increases his great sorrow in his breast longing for your return.'[4] That is what Anticleia says who herself died from longing for Odysseus.[5] But up to the time that Telemachus left for his journey to Pylus and Sparta, Laertes had in spite of his great grief for Odysseus been active supervising the work on the farm and drinking and eating with the slaves in the house whenever he wanted to. This is what Eumaeus reports to Telemachus back from his journey. But since Telemachus left, the old man—so people say—has not yet had any food or drink, nor does he see to the work, but with groaning and sighing he sits lamenting, and his skin is wasting away round his bones.[6] This is the picture of an old man who has lost all hope, since his lineage threatens to be or perhaps is already extinguished; he is close to death, from despair more than from old age. This is how Odysseus finds his father.

Laertes is alone, working the soil round a tree, a picture of abject misery, clad in patched and dirty clothes, 'increasing his grief'.[7] Like Menander's 'Self-Tormentor',[8] as Stanford says, Laertes increases his own wretchedness by the way in which he lives. When Odysseus sees him, he steps aside under a big pear tree and weeps. As he ponders what to do in view of his father's state, his first impulse is to kiss and hug him and tell him all about his coming. But then he wonders whether he should first, that is before embracing him, ask him questions and test him in everything;[9] and he decides that it would be more profitable to 'test' or 'try' him first, with 'mocking' words. It is wrong to translate *certomiois* as 'teasing' or 'bantering', because these words do not exclude friendliness or affection. But even in a relationship as close as that of Zeus to Hera and Athene the word *certomios* goes with *erethizein* 'to provoke';[10] and in each case the speech either provokes anger[11] or may provoke anger.[12] We must not be tempted into toning down what seems to us to be heartless and cruel.[13] There is here obviously a region of judgement and feeling totally different from our own. We must therefore state this strange phenomenon and try to understand it.

When Odysseus goes straight up to him, Laertes digs around the tree without looking.[14] His bodily attitude expresses his absorption in his work and also his grief.[15] Odysseus begins by praising the old man's care for the orchard. 'But,' he says, 'I will tell you something else, and do not you place anger into your heart';[16] and then proceeds to describe the old man as he appears to him without mincing matters, as uncared for, squalid, and ill-clad, while his regal looks and his size belie his slavish appearance. He concludes this part by asking whose slave he is.[17] It is obvious that all this is designed to rouse the old king to anger, which is made quite explicit.[18] Next Odysseus asks for a confirmation of whether this is really Ithaca, and then talks about a guest-friend from Ithaca, son of Laertes, whom he received hospitably in his own country, and to whom he gave a great many precious guest-gifts. The mention of Laertes' son from Ithaca is of course intended to rouse the old man's feelings. The enumeration of the many valuable gifts will be a considerable embarrassment to him, because such gifts impose the obligation of an equivalent gift in return, an obligation which Laertes in his present situation cannot fulfil. It is evident that every item in this speech is such as to harass the old man profoundly.

Laertes weeps as he replies. He confirms at once that this is Ithaca. Then follows a brief poignant description of the situation in Ithaca: it is under the control of haughty and evil men; and the man who would have returned generosity with generosity to a guest-friend is not in Ithaca. This is all defence, negative and bitter. Then Laertes moves forward with the question: how long is it since you gave hospitality to him, 'your guest, the unhappy man, my son as surely as he ever lived, a man of ill-fate?'[19] Here Laertes answers indirectly the question how he, a man of royal stature, appears like a slave, and makes it known that he is himself Laertes, the guest-friend's father. But none of it is stated explicitly; the only thing that matters is that this guest-friend was his ill-fated son who has died far from home; and the old man dwells on this, full of grief.

Odysseus answers the last question first: he stems from a place of Being-beside-oneself-with-grief, is the son of Relentless, son of Much-grief: [20] a fitting description of what lies behind him. Then he answers the previous question about how long ago the guest-friend left; and the answer is, four years ago, and with good omens, and in hope of continued guest-friendship. This answer, which brings Odysseus so near and yet leaves him so far, plunges the old man into black grief, and he strews ashes over his head. Then Odysseus himself is struck by fierce emotion, and leaping towards him he hugs and kisses him, and reveals himself, and tells him that he has slain the Suitors. In reply Laertes asks: 'If you, Odysseus, my son, have come here, tell me now a sign that is very plain so that I may be convinced.'[21] Whereupon Odysseus mentions the scar, and the trees in detail that Laertes gave him as a boy. Recognizing these signs, Laertes embraces Odysseus, and faints. But Odysseus catches him in his arms, and as he collects himself, his first word is directed to the gods: 'Father Zeus, in truth you gods still exist on great Olympus, if the Suitors have actually paid for their reckless wrongdoing.'[22] Then he immediately turns to the new terrible danger which threatens from the Suitors' kinsmen, and Odysseus leads him to the house.[23]

This encounter between Odysseus and Laertes is of course a clear example of testing in all its phases: [24] (1) the initial hesitation of Odysseus; (2) testing (type 1) by the mocking and provocative speech of Odysseus; (3) Laertes' response in his statement on affairs in Ithaca and his manifest grief; (4) Odysseus revealing himself; (5) Laertes asking for a sign (type 2 testing), and Odysseus mentioning the scar and the trees; (6) the old man fainting and Odysseus embracing him; (7) father and son going together to a meal and then to battle.

What is the point of this elaborate testing?[25] It is out of the question that the father might be disloyal to the son. But even if he were, there would be no danger for Odysseus in revealing his identity. All the same, Odysseus does not yield to his compassion for his father, but decides to test him with mocking words. The explanation for this must lie, at least in part, in what happens to Laertes. He is on the road to death from despair when Odysseus comes. Roused by the stranger's humiliating provocation, he describes the causes of his grief: the terrible injustice of the situation in Ithaca and the loss of his son. He weeps, and he strews black dust over his head with both his hands. This means that his deadly apathy is broken; he is alive again, even if he is stricken with sorrow. Told everything by Odysseus, he is cautious and slow to trust, like his son, but, given the sign, he believes, and faints with the anguish of excessive joy. As he recovers consciousness, his first word is directed to Zeus as the guardian of justice: the old king believes again in the existence of the gods because the Suitors have been punished for their transgressions; and immediately he also realises the new danger arising from the dead men's kinsfolk. It seems evident that through being tested Laertes is brought back to life and to a passionate concern for what is happening.

But this is only the first step in his regaining his stature

as the old king. He is bathed, dresses well, is enhanced by
Athene, and admired by his son. He wishes he could have been
young enough to share in the battle against the Suitors.[26] He
glories in seeing his son and son's son compete with each
other in valour;[27] and in the end Athene fulfils his longing for
a part in the fight. She 'breathes great power' into him, and
he kills Eupeithes, father of Antinous, the leading and the
worst Suitor, who was himself killed by the first shot of
Odysseus. With this success in battle Laertes is fully restored
to heroic stature: he is rejuvenated, even as Telemachus has
grown to the stature of manhood.

The importance of Laertes and his full recovery as a hero
becomes evident when the place of kin in the Homeric world
is taken into account. According to Finley, 'the profundity of
the Greeks' kinship attachment, throughout their history, is
immediately apparent from their passion for genealogies.'[28]
This is, for instance, apparent in the usual introduction of a
hero by his father's name in addition to his own name. He
may often be called 'the son of so-and-so'. Even if kinship is
not the primary tie in Homeric society, it is one of the
strongest.[29] There is a general emphasis on the family in the
*Odyssey*. Quite apart from descriptions of family life in
Ithaca, Pylus, Sparta and Scheria, it appears in comparisons
and similes where it is rich in warmth and humanity.[30] But as
important and more specific is the relationship between father,
son and son's son, the representatives of a noble line. Just as
Odysseus in the Underworld asks his mother about his father
and his son, so Achilles asks Odysseus about Neleus, his
father, and his son Neoptolemus, and is delighted to hear of
his son's excellence.[31] From the same point of view, Penelope
calls Telemachus the offspring of Laertes and Odysseus, which
shows how the royal line of Arcisius is represented by the
three ages: the old man, the man, and the young man.[32] The
pride of noble lineage appears most clearly when Odysseus
warns Telemachus 'not to shame the race of us the fathers who
have been famous for valour and manliness all over the
earth.'[33] This final glorification of the lineage of Odysseus is
only possible when Laertes, his father, has been fully rein-
stated as a hero.

# CONCLUSION

# THE STRUCTURE OF THE ODYSSEY

Homer's image for an epic poem is a 'path' (*oime*).[1] 'When they had satisfied their desire for food and drink, the Muse sent forth the singer to sing the fame of men, from the "path" (*i.e.* epic)—the fame of which then reached the broad sky —the quarrel between Odysseus and Achilles, son of Peleus.'[2] This quarrel is, according to Stanford, an episode from a famous epic or 'path'. When the singer begins his song, he is sent forth by the Muse: he speeds along the path of his song. When the bard turns from one subject of song to another, he 'changes his walk'. Odysseus, asking Demodocus to sing a different song, says to him: 'But now change your walk and sing of the arrangement of the Wooden Horse which Epeius made with Athene.'[3] The singers are honoured, 'because the Muse teaches them paths'; and Phemius in self-defence says to Odysseus: 'A god has made to grow in my mind varied paths.'[4] The singer in action is imagined as a man speeding along a path. Here the 'path' implies the direction the walker takes. The path therefore is the 'plan' or the 'arrangement of events', as the Yugoslav bards would call it.[5]

Let us try to describe the 'path' of the *Odyssey*. We have already seen that the *Odyssey* is, like the *Iliad,* from the point of view of length best arranged in six groups of four books. The singing of each group is a 'lap' in the singer's movement along the path of his poem. Each 'lap' has, as I hope to show, a rhythm and structure of its own.[6]

The theme of the *Odyssey* is Odysseus, as the first line of the epic tells us. If this is kept firmly in mind, the 'laps' of the path along which the singer moves emerge readily. During the first twelve books Odysseus is abroad; during the second twelve he is, after a brief farewell and journey, in Ithaca. In Books 1 to 4 Odysseus is not encountered in person, but others, like Athene, Nestor, Menelaus, and most of all Telemachus, think and speak of him. In Books 5 to 8 Odysseus appears, described by the poet, first on Calypso's island and then in Phaeacia. In Books 9 to 12, Odysseus himself relates his own wanderings. In Books 13 to 16 Odysseus lands on Ithaca and stays at Eumaeus' hut. In Books 17 to 20 he stays in the palace at Ithaca under the disguise of an old beggar. In Books 21 to 24 he regains his power.

Let us consider each 'lap' in turn with a view to understanding its structure. While each has many connections with what precedes and what follows, each one is also a well-knit composition.

The first 'lap' (Books 1 to 4) is outlined by Athene's plan.[7] While providing for Hermes going to Calypso in order to tell her to release Odysseus in the second 'lap', it determines the action of the first 'lap' in detail. Athene will put 'power' into the heart of Telemachus and rouse him to action (Book 1) so that he will call an assembly and in public denounce the Suitors (Book 2a). She will send him off by ship (Book 2b) to Sparta (Book 4) and Pylus (Book 3) in order to gain fame for himself and to seek news of his father. This leads to the homecomings told by Nestor and Menelaus, and the disclosure that Odysseus is alive, but captive of Calypso. The main dramatic theme of the first 'lap' is the initiation by Athene of Telemachus' growing-up, and its first stages: in his self-assertion against his mother and the Suitors in the palace (Book 1), before the people of Ithaca in the public assembly, in his first command of a ship (Book 2), and in his travels abroad to Pylus and Sparta (Books 3 and 4).[8] The counter-theme to Telemachus and his development are the Suitors and their increasing evil-doing. Their sin and punishment is foreshadowed by Zeus' thoughts about Aegisthus, his crime and his death.[9] Their evil intentions are still wrapped up in courtesy in the speeches of Antinous and Eurymachus in Book 1.

They become plainer in their speeches in the public assembly (Book 2). They form into the plan to murder Telemachus in Book 4, which ends with the Suitors lying in ambush for him on the island of Asteris.[10]

The second 'lap' (Books 5 to 8) is outlined by Zeus' command to Hermes. While Zeus tells Athene to bring Telemachus safely back to Ithaca (Book 15) and let the Suitors' ambush be in vain (Book 16), he gives Hermes a detailed message for Calypso: Odysseus must travel wretchedly on a raft without safe-conduct of gods and men from Ogygia until on the twentieth day he arrives in Scheria of the Phaeacians, who will honour him like a god, take him home and give him many presents.[11] The dramatic theme of the second 'lap' is the contrast between Ogygia and Scheria, the transition from the enforced concealment on Calypso's island to the free hospitality of the Phaeacians who take strangers home, from the temptation of seven years of living with a goddess to the brief meeting with Nausicaa whose very name suggests the homeward bound ship.[12]

The third 'lap' (Books 9 to 12) consists of the wanderings of Odysseus told by the hero himself in reply to Alcinous' questions about his identity and travels. The common theme of these tales is Odysseus' heroic valour and intelligence with which he overcomes all obstacles. The tales are, as we have seen, arranged concentrically around Odysseus' visit to the Underworld.[13]

In the fourth 'lap' (Books 13 to 16) the dramatic theme is the converging and meeting of Odysseus and Telemachus, Odysseus arriving from Phaeacia in Book 13 and going to Eumaeus' hut in Book 14, and Telemachus arriving on Ithaca from Sparta in Book 15 and going to Eumaeus' hut where he meets Odysseus in Book 16. This is clearly set out by Athene when she plans future action with Odysseus.[14]

It might be objected that the fourth 'lap' cannot be said to begin at the beginning of Book 13, because the Phaeacian tale is not finished. There is, however, no point in the book where the poet has marked off the Phaeacian episode from Odysseus' arrival in Ithaca; the two are dovetailed in such a way that they are inseparable. The poet finally leaves the Phaeacians in the first part of line 187, and describes Odysseus as waking up in his own country in the second part of that line. The fate of the Phaeacians is clearly intended to be understood in close connection with what happens to Odysseus in Book 13. We shall return to this presently. Also, the unity of the third 'lap' (Books 9 to 12), told in the first person by Odysseus himself, would be destroyed by the addition of a group of lines from Book 13 told in the third person.[15] Finally, the last and greatest guest-gift, farewell and departure from abroad belong together with the arrival on Ithaca in Book 13, as they do in the case of Telemachus in Book 15.

In the fifth 'lap' (Books 17 to 20), Odysseus follows Telemachus to the palace in the guise of a beggar and joins the household in order to explore the situation. From the Suitors he encounters violence regularly. In Book 17, Melantheus, goatherd and partisan of Eurymachus, kicks the beggar and tells him that stools will be flung at him; Antinous threatens to do it, and finally hurls a stool which hits Odysseus.[16] This is the climax; the subsequent acts of violence are less effective. In Book 18, Eurymachus hurls a stool at the beggar, but Odysseus sits down and a cupbearer is struck and falls to the ground.[17] In Book 20, Ctesippus hurls an ox foot, but misses Odysseus and hits the wall.[18] Odysseus also finds out which of the maids and which of his men are loyal to him. He is recognized by the old dog Argus and by Eurycleia, but he is not recognized by Penelope. His encounter with her is a major theme. In Book 17, she invites the beggar through Eumaeus. In Book 19, he meets her and tests her.[19] Finally, the fifth 'lap' begins and ends with a prophecy of Theoclymenus.[20]

In the sixth 'lap' (Books 21 to 24), Odysseus regains his supremacy in Ithaca and is restored to his family. When Penelope fetches the bow for the Suitors' contest, this is the 'beginning of the killing.'[21] The bow contest (Book 21) leads to the battle with the Suitors and their death (Book 22). After the battle Odysseus is reunited with Penelope (Book 23).[22] Reunited also with his father Laertes,[23] Odysseus fights a brief battle with the Suitors' kinsmen until Zeus brings about peace.

The simplicity with which the abundant material of this epic is organized in these six 'laps' is striking. It is quite easy to give appropriate titles to each 'lap':

1. Telemachus against the Suitors, and abroad.
2. Odysseus with Calypso and in Phaeacia.
3. Odysseus' wanderings.
4. Meeting of Odysseus and Telemachus on Ithaca in Eumaeus' hut.
5. Odysseus as a beggar in his palace.
6. Odysseus restored to supremacy, and reunited with Penelope and Laertes.

This, together with the brief contents of each 'lap', is the 'plan' or the 'arrangement of the events' or the 'path', as Homer would call it, which the bard makes his own when he learns a new song. A path gives direction to him who walks it: the events of a story are given in tradition to a singer. A path is also made by him who walks it: the events of a story may be rearranged by a singer. Whether strictly traditional or somewhat altered, the song is to Homer a path which directs his movements in his singing. To fulfil this function, the 'path' or plan of the poem must be simple, and so it is in the *Odyssey,* as we have seen.

But beyond this there is also in the *Odyssey* a basic idea or image which controls and pervades the whole of the poem. What it is has to some extent been indicated by Aristotle. Dividing epic poetry into the same species as tragedy, Aristotle says that the *Odyssey* is complex in structure, because it is 'discovery' throughout.[25] *Anagnorisis* is 'discovery' or 'recognition' or 'getting to know', in fact, 'a change from ignorance to knowledge', as Aristotle puts it. These terms are fitting for an abstract analysis like Aristotle's *Poetics,* but they would be of little use as a guiding theme for a singer. Now Uvo Hölscher has described 'concealment' and 'disclosure' as the basic ideas of the homecoming of Odysseus.[26] The two terms mean much the same thing as *anagnorisis,* but they are nearer to a gesture or an image, and in consequence much more flexible and more adequate to such stuff as poetry is.

It is not difficult to see that 'concealment' and 'disclosure'—

which are of course complementary to each other—are the
dramatic ideas on which the second half of the *Odyssey* is
built. We will come back to this presently. But for the first
half it is hardly satisfactory to say, as Hermann does,[27] that
Telemachus is recognized by Nestor, Menelaus and Helen, and
Odysseus by the Cyclopes and the Phaeacians. It is true, of
course, but too fragmented to guide composition of half an
epic.

We have however already met a figure embodying the idea
of 'concealment': Calypso, the 'Concealer'. She is described
by Homer in Book 5 only, but significant references to her
span Books 1 to 12. The concealment which is the work of
Calypso is exclusively concerned with Odysseus, whom she
desires to keep in Ogygia. The 'recognition' of Telemachus
by Nestor, and by Menelaus and Helen, is therefore a second-
ary and subordinate theme. It is, as we have seen, ornamental
within the theme of guest-friendship.[28]

After the prooemium of the first book, Homer explains the
situation: all the other heroes who have escaped death are at
home; Odysseus alone is held back by the 'Concealer', who
wants him to be her husband. In the divine assembly which
follows, Athene explains in more detail the pitiful position
of Odysseus, longing for home, but unable to leave Ogygia.
The outcome is that Zeus agrees to Athene's twofold pro-
posal: first, that Hermes is to travel to Ogygia and convey
Zeus' order to the 'Concealer' that she must release Odysseus;
and secondly, that Athene is to inspire Telemachus both to
oppose the Suitors and to go on a journey in order to seek
news about his father. Both these proposals are designed to
lift the veil of Odysseus' concealment. When Telemachus in
Book 1 says that the gods 'made Odysseus unseen', which may
also suggest 'given over to destruction', and that 'he has gone
out of sight and out of all possibility of enquiry', he describes
how in fact he is concealed from his family.[29] The goal of
Telemachus' journey is reached when in Book 4 Menelaus
tells him of his meeting with Proteus, who had seen Odysseus
'on an island shedding ample tears in the house of the nymph
Calypso who keeps him back by compulsion; and he cannot
reach his native land.'[30] Telemachus knows at last that his

father is alive, but his whereabouts are still hidden. In Book 5, Odysseus' release from the power of the 'Concealer' is described. Here Calypso is much more than a 'concealing force'; she is, as we have seen, a beautiful, divine woman who loves Odysseus.[31] But, as Penelope is wooed by the Suitors and resists them out of loyalty for Odysseus, so Odysseus is wanted by Calypso but resists out of loyalty to Penelope. In Book 7, Odysseus is asked by Arete, queen of the Phaeacians, where he has come from, and he describes his arrival at Ogygia, how Calypso cared for him, and his voyage from there to Scheria.[32] In Book 9, Odysseus, introducing the full recital of his wanderings, declares his name and describes his native island, Ithaca, concluding with the words: 'In truth, there is nothing lovelier for me to see than my own country.'[33] By way of contrast he mentions Calypso, who wanted him for her husband; and he mentions Circe, who also wanted him for her husband, but never persuaded his heart in his breast. This is the beginning of Odysseus' tale. His tale ends with his arrival at Ogygia and Calypso's care for him. Then he breaks off, because he has told them about Calypso before.

The recurrent motif of Calypso, the 'Concealer' of Odysseus, permeates the first half of the *Odyssey*. She is also the last of his adventures before his arrival in Phaeacia, and in a way she is the culmination and epitome of *all* his adventures because in each one he is either threatened by death or tempted to stay.

The transition from the 'Concealer' to Ithaca is accomplished by way of the Phaeacians, who in their capacity of *pompoi* take Odysseus to his own land.[34] In this transitional part the idea of concealment and disclosure is expressed by a variety of images. The strangely intelligent ships of the Phaeacians travel 'concealed in mist and cloud'.[35] They travel by night. Odysseus watches for the setting of the sun so that they may depart, and as the morning star rises, which announces the light of early-born Dawn, the ship approaches Ithaca.[36] Here mist, cloud, and the darkness of night conceal the ship and Odysseus from others so that no harm can befall them.[37] With the dawn the Phaeacians deposit Odysseus fast asleep on the shore of Ithaca. Then they return to Scheria, but as they approach their harbour Poseidon, angry because they have taken Odysseus home, turns the ship into rock and roots it at the bottom of the sea, thus fulfilling an ancient oracle.[38] The rock-nature of the ship and its rootedness are images of the ship's immobility. What this means is expressed plainly by Alcinous when he says to his anxious people: 'Let us then all act in obedience to my words: cease from escorting home anyone who comes to our city. But let us sacrifice twelve choice bulls to Poseidon, if he perhaps may pity us, and not conceal us round about by a huge mountain.' While in the past the Phaeacians have been the safe 'escorters' of men from the concealment of far lands to the known presence of their own land and family, they are so no longer. For men longing to get home their ships will be immobile, like a rock rooted at the bottom of the sea. It is even possible that Poseidon will close up their city by a mighty mountain.[39] By these images and the words of Alcinous the realm of strange and distant seas and islands is firmly blocked off and concealed for ever.

But the concealment of Odysseus is not lifted, either immediately or wholly. The images of concealment are many: mist hides Odysseus from any chance arrival; it also hides Ithaca from Odysseus; disguise hides Athene from Odysseus; a fictitious tale is intended to hide Odysseus from the stranger who is Athene. Mist, disguise, and lies are all means of concealment: they continue the work of Calypso, but are suspended while Athene and Odysseus meet.[40]

They plan the future course of action, and Athene proposes that she will make Odysseus unrecognizable by turning him into an old man in beggar's clothes. She does this by touching him with her staff and clothing him in rags. Through this transformation Odysseus is once again concealed, a concealment which he has to uphold of course by fictitious tales. The function of Odysseus' fictitious tales is to conceal him, and in addition they often serve to test the listening person.[41]

In the course of the second half of the epic the veil of concealment is lifted gradually. Athene turns Odysseus into his former self so that Telemachus may accept him as his father.[42] It is not possible of course for Telemachus to 'recognize' his father, because he himself was a babe in arms when Odysseus left. It is the miracle of the transformation and Odysseus' explanation that this is the work of Athene which convince the young man that this is his father. Here, the transformation is dramatically necessary; a mere disguise and change through time would have been ineffective. When Eumaeus returns, Athene transforms Odysseus again into an old beggar so that the swineherd may not recognize him.[43]

After this, the veil of concealment becomes steadily thinner. Eurycleia remarks on the beggar's similarity to Odysseus in build, voice and feet and then recognizes him by the scar on his thigh.[44] In this situation, a 'transformed' Odysseus would not have been *recognized,* even if he had the scar. One can properly 'recognize' only what one has met before. By sheer necessity, 'transformation' becomes change through age, in the context.[45] In his battle with Irus, Odysseus has his own mighty frame,[46] and of course also in the battle with the Suitors. In the end, Odysseus suggests, perhaps half ironically, that Penelope still does not believe that he is Odysseus, because he is dirty and clothed in tatters.[47] When he is bathed and beautified by Athene it is only the suffering of twenty years and Penelope's fear of being deceived that retards full recognition. Laertes has of course long ago stopped hoping for Odysseus' return. The passage of time and the old man's apathy, together with Odysseus' fictitious tale, are sufficient to conceal his identity.

To sum up, the idea which controls the *Odyssey* as a whole is, as U. Hölscher says, 'concealment and its complement "disclosure"'. In the first half of the epic the idea of concealment is embodied in the person of Calypso. By returning to her again and again throughout the first half of the epic, the poet indicates how Odysseus is hidden away beyond unknown seas. In Book 13, Homer lets veil after veil fall from the eyes of Odysseus himself; and in the second half of the epic he represents him as emerging from his concealment, step by step, as one after the other of his own people, his enemies, and last of all his wife and his father recognize him.

# NOTES

## NOTES ON INTRODUCTION

1. J. A. Davison, 'The Transmission of the Text', *Companion to Homer,* p. 219.
2. J. A. Davison, 'Thucydides, Homer and the "Achaean Wall" ', *Greek, Roman and Byzantine Studies,* vol. 6 (1965) No. 1, pp. 23-7. I owe reference to this article to my colleague, Associate Professor J. R. Hamilton. For the belief that the traditional division into books of the Homeric epics is ancient cf. A. Lesky, *A History of Greek Literature* (London, 1966), pp. 23-4.
3. Davison, op. cit., p. 23, n. 25.
4. A. B. Lord, 'Composition by Theme in Epos', *TAPA* 82 (1951) p. 74.
5. Lord, loc. cit.
6. Plato, *Repl.* 3 394 c; cf. A. Lesky, op. cit., p. 65.
7. Aristotle, *Poetics* 1460 a 5 ff.; cf. H. D. F. Kitto, *Poiesis* (Sather Class. Lect. 36, 1966) p. 150; C. M. Bowra, 'Composition' in *Companion to Homer,* p. 66.

## NOTES ON CHAPTER I

# THE HOMECOMINGS OF THE ACHAEANS

1. *Od.* 1.32 ff.
2. *Od.* 2.246 ff.
3. Hildebrecht Hommel, 'Aigisthos und die Freier. Zum Poetischen Plan und zum geschichtlichen Ort der Odyssee', *Studium Generale* 8 (1955) Heft 4; Howard W. Clarke, *The Art of the Odyssey* (Spectrum Book, U.S.A. 1967), pp. 10 ff.
4. *Od.* i.37 ff.; cf. Hommel, op cit., p. 241.
5. E. R. Dodds, *The Greeks and the Irrational* (University of California Press, 1951), p. 32.
6. *Od.* 1.227, 229.
7. *Od.* 1.368.
8. ὑπέρβιον ὕβριν ἔχοντες *Od.* 4.321; ὕβριν ἔχοντες 4.627 = 17.169; ὑβρίζοντες ἀτάσθαλα μηχανόωνται 3.207 = 17.588 = 20.370 (second person plural) = 18.143 (without ὑβρίζοντες). Cf. also Tiresias κείνων γε βίας ἀποτίσεαι ἐλθών, 11.118; beggar Odysseus about the Suitors τῶν ὕβρις τε βίη τε σιδήρεον οὐρανὸν ἵκει 17.565.
9. *Od.* 17.487. Cf. Stanford ad loc., and V. Ehrenberg, *Aspects of the Ancient World* (Oxford, 1946) p. 75 on *Eunomie.*
10. *Od.* 22.64.

11. *Od*. 22.413 and 416; cf. also Laertes 24.351-2, and Halitherses in the second Ithacan assembly 24.455-60.
12. *Od*. 24.484-5; H. D. F. Kitto, *Poiesis* (University of California Press, 1966), pp. 139-40 has shown that Odysseus' battle with the Suitors' kinsmen is a necessary part of the epic.
13. Hommel, op. cit., p. 243. But cf. Albin Lesky, *Anzeiger f.d. Altertumswissenschaft* 8, 3 (1955), p. 155.
14. *Od*. 1.298 ff., 3.195 ff.
15. *Od*. 11.441 ff., esp. 455-6.
16. *Od*. 13.383-5; he actually knew about the Suitors already through Tiresias (11.115 ff.), but it would have been pointless and tactless to mention this to Athene: he speaks as if he owed *all* his security to her.
17. For detail on his transformation, disguise, etc. cf. Conclusion, p. 128.
18. *Od*. 24.3-4; cf. 5.47-8.
19. *Od*. 7.136-8.
20. *Il*. 14.231.
21. *Il*. 16.672 ff.
22. *Il*. 2.302 οὖς μὴ κῆρες ἔβαν φέρουσαι; *Od*. 14.207-8 τὸν κῆρες ἔβαν θανάτοιο φέρουσαι εἰς ᾿Αίδαο δόμους. Both these passages are quoted by Page, p. 132, n. 17. His statement that the line from the Odyssey may be a 'misunderstanding' of the line in the Iliad is an unwarranted destruction of good evidence.—According to Page, p. 131, n. 15 the epithet κυλλήνιος occurs for Hermes from the early sixth century on, but not in Homer except for our passage. This epithet is however likely to be very old. The name Hermes occurs on a Pylus tablet. Cyllene is a mountain in Arcadia, and Hermes is associated with other Arcadian places (L. R. Farnell, *The Cults of the Greek States,* Oxford, 1909, vol. 5, pp. 3-4). The dialect of Arcadia is descended from or at least closely related to Mycenaean Greek. This makes it probable that Cyllenian Hermes was in fact a Mycenaean god, and so given to our poet in his tradition.—The original name of the city of *Cyllene* was *Mecone,* meaning 'Poppytown' which connects with Hermes as a god of sleep (E. A. S. Butterworth, *Some Traces of the Pre-Olympian World in Greek Literature and Myth,* Berlin, 1966, pp. 175 and 154, n. 80).
23. *Od*. 24.205 ff.
24. *Od*. 1.82 ff.
25. *Od*. 11.626; cf. also Farnell, op. cit., vol. 5, p. 5 on the tradition that in the temple of Athene Polias on the Acropolis there was an ancient *agalma* of Hermes dedicated by

Cecrops. The connection with Cecrops suggests that the association of Athene and Hermes goes back to Mycenaean times.

26. The stages of this journey, apart from 'ocean', are not met with elsewhere in Homer in exactly the same form. But the 'White Rock' reminds one of the rock at the confluence of the two rivers in *Od*. 10.515. The 'Gates of the Sun' correspond to Circe's island 'where there is the house and the dancing-floor of early-born Dawn and the place of the rising of the Sun' 12.3-4. 'The land' or 'district of dreams' derives from the sort of imagery out of which Penelope speaks of the two Gates of Dreams 19.562 ff. These mythical places are not as foreign to Homer as Page maintains (p. 118).

27. *Od*. 20.355-6; cf. chapter VI, p. 62.
28. *Od*. 22.383 ff.
29. *Od*. 22.448-50.
30. *Od*. 24.1 and 5; it would be very strange if the spirits of the Suitors suddenly started to set off for Hades themselves, as Page's suggestion (p. 117) that they should fly to Hades without a guide implies.
31. *Od*. 24.19.
32. *Od*. 3.109 ff., 11.467 ff.
33. *Od*. 24.98 ff.
34. *Od*. 24.15 ff. and 99 ff.; cf. Page, p. 119 on the difficulties of this passage.
35. *Od*. 24.15; cf. Walter Arend, *Die typischen Szenen bei Homer, Problemata* 7, Berlin 1933, pp. 28-34.
36. Cunliffe, s.v. εὑρίσκω
37. *Il*. 2.169 ff.
38. *Il*. 3.125 ff.
39. *Il*. 9.186 ff.; cf. also *Il*. 4.327 ff., 365 ff., 18.3 ff.; this form of presentation is an 'appositional expansion', cf. H. and A. Thornton, *Time and Style* (Dunedin and London, 1962). Chapter 1.
40. *Il*. 4.293; in this case the verb is ἔτετμε.
41. *Od*. 4.3 ff.
42. *Od*. 4.6 and 13.
43. *Od*. 5.151 ff.
44. For movement backward into the past in an 'appositional expansion', cf. H. and A. Thornton, op. cit., pp. 3, 4, 7 etc.
45. *Od*. 24.15.
46. *Od*. 24.99-100.
47. That Achilles is the leader of the group in lines 15 ff. is indicated by line 9: 'Thus they were gathered round him'; cf. also 11.467 ff.; for the connection of these two passages cf. Webster, p. 260.

48. When Aristarchus calls the dialogue ἄκαιρος which means 'ill-timed, unseasonable', he probably refers to this chronological difficulty.
49. The charge of irrelevance directed against the first conversation arises from considering it in isolation; cf. Stanford on *Od*. 24.23 ff., Page, pp. 118-9, Kirk, p. 249.
50. *Od*. 24.98 and 203-4.
51. *Od*. 3.93; cf. Howard W. Clarke, op. cit., pp. 62-3. But the glory of Odysseus is as great as that of Achilles, if not greater, because his intelligence conquered Troy in the end.
52. *Od*. 8.74 ff.; cf. chapter III, p. 43.
53. *Od*. 11.482-6.
54. *Od*. 24.95.
55. *Od*. 11.441 ff.
56. *Od*. 24.196 ff.
57. Cf. U. Hölscher, 'Untersuchungen zur Form der Odyssee', *Hermes*, Einzelschriften 6, 1939, p. 21.
58. W. G. Anderson, 'Calypso and Elysium' in *Essays on the Odyssey*.
59. *Od*. 1.326-7.
60. The phrase νόστον..λυγρόν, which occurs in 1.326-7 and in 3.135 suggests that the 'grievous homecoming' as told by Menelaus and the others is in fact the content of the bard's song; cf. also Athene's anger mentioned in both passages.
61. *Od*. 3.132-6.
62. *Od*. 3.184-5.
63. *Od*. 3.255 ff.
64. *Od*. 3.261.
65. καὶ κεῖνος *Od*. 3.286, *i.e.* like Nestor before him.
66. Cf. W. Schadewaldt, *Iliasstudien* (Darmstadt, 1966), p. 119 and p. 85, note 2.
67. *Od*. 3.303; cf. also 4.90-1.
68. *Od*. 4.81 ff.
69. *Od*. 4.349 ff.
70. *Od*. 3.311.
71. *Od*. 3.300.
72. *Od*. 4.83.
73. *Od*. 11.409 ff.
74. *Od*. 4.535.
75. *Od*. 11.420.
76. *Od*. 22.309 and 24.185.
77. Cf. also 24.96-7.
78. *Od*. 8.491.
79. Cf. Albin Lesky, 'Die Schuld der Klytaimnestra', *Wiener Studien*, Neue Folge, Bd. 1 (80. Band) 1967, pp. 11 ff.

NOTES ON CHAPTER II

# THE WANDERINGS OF ODYSSEUS

1. *Od*. 5.151 ff., cf. 82-3.
2. *Od*. 7.259.
3. *Od*. 5.32 ff.
4. *Od*. 5.140 ff.
5. *Od*. 5.262 ff.
6. *Od*. 8.566.
7. *Od*. 8.562 ff.
8. *Od*. 1.14 f., 56 f.
9. *Od*. 5.155.
10. *Od*. 5.130 ff.
11. *Od*. 5.116.
12. *Od*. 5.161, 191.
13. *Od*. 5.209-10.
14. *Od*. 5.153.
15. W. J. Woodhouse, *The Composition of Homer's Odyssey* (Oxford, 1930), pp. 57 ff., and Stanford on *Od*. 8.457 ff.
16. *Od*. 6.153 ff.
17. *Od*. 6.244-5.
18. *Od*. 6.290, 313-5.
19. *Od*. 7.315.
20. *Od*. 8.461-2.
21. *Od*. 9.39 ff. and 196 ff.
22. *Od*. 9.92 ff.
23. *Od*. 9.105 ff.
24. *Od*. 10.80 ff.; cf. Karl Meuli in *R.E.*, s.v. *Laistrygonen*, Suppl. V, 538 f. (1931).
25. *Od*. 6.4-5.
26. *Od*. 6.204-5; cf. 279.
27. *Od*. 7.205-6; cf. also 5.35 = 19.279.
28. *Od*. 9.529.
29. *Od*. 7.56 ff.
30. *Od*. 10.21.
31. *Od*. 10.138-9.
32. *Od*. 12.3-4.
33. *Od*. 12.263.
34. *Od*. 11.14 ff.
35. *Od*. 12.61 ff., cf. Kirk, pp. 234-5; cf. also Stuart Piggott, 'Heads and Hoofs', *Antiquity* 36, 1962, p. 114, who connects the Golden Fleece with shamanic offerings of skins or hides.
36. H. M. and N. K. Chadwick, *The Growth of Literature*, vol. III (Cambridge, 1940), pp. 702-3.
37. Cf. also Chadwick, op. cit., p. 744.
38. Cf. Chadwick, op. cit., p. 731; cf. Webster, pp. 123, 171.

39. Karl Meuli, 'Scythica', *Hermes* 70 (1935) pp. 167 ff.; cf. also Alfred Heubeck, 'Fachbericht' on Homer, *Gymnasium* 66, 1959, p. 402 who connects with shamanism features of the figure of Odysseus to which Rhys Carpenter has drawn attention in his *Folk Tale, Fiction and Saga in the Homeric Epics* (University of California Press, 1946). Older literature mentioned by Meuli.

40. Mircea Eliade, *Shamanism: Archaic Techniques of Ecstasy* (Paris, 1951; transl. London, 1964).

41. For the question of when shamanic material entered Greek culture cf. p. 36 below and note 133.

42. Eliade, p. 8.

43. Eliade, p. 5.

44. E.g. cf. Eliade, pp. 210-1.

45. Cf. Chadwick, op. cit., vol III, p. 199.

46. A. B. Lord, *The Singer of Tales* (Harvard Univ. Press, 1960) *passim;* references to Milman Parry on pp. 3 and 11.

47. Eliade, p. 214.

48. *Od*. 15.285.

49. *Od*. 13.79-80.

50. An independent piece of evidence for this is found in Plutarch's *Moralia* 27 E: 'The Etruscans preserve a tradition that Odysseus was by nature sleepy (ὑπνώδους) and for that reason difficult to approach for the majority of people'. Carl Kerenyi, who quotes this passage, rightly to my mind, rejects the possibility that the Etruscan story might be derived from the *Odyssey* on the grounds that Odysseus is nowhere in the *Odyssey* represented as unapproachable (Erich Lessing, *The Voyages of Ulysses,* Macmillan, 1966, pp. 249-50). But I do not share Kerenyi's belief that Odysseus was originally a 'god of nature'; therefore the sleep of the Hittite fertility god Telepinus does not seem to me to be comparable with the sleep of Odysseus. The Etruscan tradition suggests that the sleeping of Odysseus was something outside the ordinary. Cf. also the Etruscan mirror described on p. 25 of this chapter.

51. Cf. Stanford on *Od*. 9.39-40; Webster, p. 123.

52. *Od*. 9.196 ff.

53. Cf. Eliade, pp. 387 ff.; E. R. Dodds, *The Greeks and the Irrational* (University of California Press, 1951), pp. 140 ff.

54. Herodotus 4.13; J. D. P. Bolton in his *Aristeas of Proconnesus* (Oxford, 1962) denies the shamanic character of Aristeas; but W. Burkert in his review of the book refutes this, rightly I think (*Gnomon* 35, 1963, pp. 238 ff.).

55. Herodotus 4.36.

56. Cf. Dodds, op. cit., p. 141 and p. 161, n. 36 ff.

57. Diels-Kranz, *Fragmente der Vorsokratiker* (Dublin, Zürich, 1966) vol. 1, Pythag. A 7; Dodds, op. cit., p. 166, n. 63.
58. W. K. C. Guthrie, *The Greeks and their Gods* (London, 1950), p. 195.
59. Quoted by C. M. Bowra, *Heroic Poetry* (London, 1964), p. 19, n. 4 from J. D. Beazley, *JHS* 69, 1949, p. 5 and Plate IV a.
60. Neither Bowra nor Beazley mentions the jug.
61. *Il.* 1.72.
62. Eliade, pp. 64, 84 tobacco juice, p. 130 *takini* plant among the Caribs of Dutch Guiana, p. 221 mushrooms in Siberia, p. 399 hemp smoke in ancient Iran; also 'a mixture of wine and "narcotic of Vishtap"' which put Artay Viraf to sleep for seven days and nights. Professor T. B. L. Webster has suggested to me that the shamanic narcotic in Mycenaean times might have been opium which is well attested. According to Eliade p. 402, n. 118, opium was used 'in certain Persian mystical orders'. Cf. also E. A. S. Butterworth, *Some Traces of the Pre-Olympian World in Greek Literature and Myth* (Berlin, 1966), p. 155.
63. Eliade, pp. 208 ff.
64. *Od.* 11.52.
65. *Od.* 7.259.
66. *Od.* 1.50.
67. *Od.* 1.52-4.
68. In the first case ὅθι refers back to νήσῳ ἐν ἀμφιρύτῃ, and νῆσος δενδρήεσσα 51 is either an anacoluthon (Merry and Riddell) or a new sentence lacking the copula (Stanford); but it is also possible to take the ὅθι-clause as parallel to νήσῳ ἐν ἀμφιρύτῃ, both describing the place where Odysseus is suffering grief; then νῆσος δενδρήεσσα 51 would be in apposition to ὄμφαλος θαλάσσης: the island full of trees would stand out from the sea, as the navel from the belly or the boss from the surface of a shield; cf. Eustathius ad loc. 1389. 30-2.
69. Eliade, p. 259.
70. The *omphalos* is of course a 'centre' of this sort; cf. Eliade, p. 268.
71. Hesiod, *Theogony* 805-6.
72. Cf. on this and the following Hermann Güntert's suggestions in his *Kalypso* quoted by William S. Anderson in 'Calypso and Elysium', *Essays on the Odyssey*, pp. 81-2. Both these scholars believe that Calypso, Ogygia and so on are connected with death; and Anderson argues that as Menelaus lives uneasily towards an unsatisfactory Elysium, so Odysseus moves away from an unsatisfactory Ogygia into a full life of action. If this interpretation is correct, the original

shamanic otherwordliness of Calypso has been used by the poet for his composition.

73. *Od.* 1.52-4.
74. Hesiod, *Theogony* 746-7; cf. also 517-9.
75. Cf. R.E., s.v. *Atlas* vol. 2 (1896), 2129 ff.
76. Aeschylus, *Prometheus* 349-50, cf. 425 ff.
77. *Herodotus* 4.184.
78. R. W. Macan, *Herodotus* (London, 1895) ad loc.; Virgil has beautifully combined the ideas of the great mountain and the person of Atlas, *Aeneid* 4.246 ff.
79. Pindar, *Pyth.* 1.19.
80. Schol. Aeschylus, *Prom.* 428; Schol. Eurip. *Hipp.* 747 (Schwartz); Eustath. *Od.* 1.52 (1389, 59).
81. Eliade, pp. 260-1.
82. Eliade, p. 266.
83. Eliade, p. 265.
84. Stanford on *Od.* 1.54.
85. Hesiod, *Theogony* 507 ff.
86. Eliade, p. 267.
87. Eliade, p. 172.
88. *Od.* 7.259.
89. Eliade, pp. 274 ff.
90. Eliade, p. 278.
91. Herodotus 4.14.3.
92. Hesiod, *Erga* 383.
93. Eliade, pp. 168 ff.
94. Eliade, p. 173.
95. Eliade, p. 174.
96. Cf. *Od.* 21.411 where the bow-string is said to sing beautifully like a swallow.
97. Eliade, p. 175, n. 140; cf. the arrow carried by the shaman Abaris round the world, Herodotus 4.36.
98. Eliade, p. 172.
99. *Od.* 5.28 ff.
100. For 'giant fir tree' cf. Eliade, pp. 37, 270.
101. *Od.* 5.238-40.
102. Eliade, p. 271.
103. *Od.* 5.63 ff.
104. *Od.* 1.15.
105. *Od.* 5.136.
106. Eliade, pp. 76-7.
107. *Od.* 5.194 ff.
108. Cf. Gabriel Germain. *Genèse de l'Odyssée* (Paris, 1954), p. 333; Webster, p. 247; Fr. Eichhorn, *Homers Odyssee, Ein Führer durch die Dichtung* (Göttingen, 1965), pp. 63-4; cf.

also W. Schadewaldt, 'Der Helioszorn in der Odyssee', *Studi in onore di L. Castiglioni* (Florence, 1960), p. 863.

109. W. K. C. Guthrie, *A History of Greek Philosophy* (Cambridge, 1965), vol. 2, p. 11.

110. Pliny, *N.H.* 7.174.

111. Diels-Kranz, op. cit., Epimenides, fr. 1 ad fin.

112. But cf. Guthrie, op. cit., p. 10, n. 2 for parallels drawn between the *Odyssey* and the prooemium of Parmenides.

113. It is possible that the similes of the four-horse chariot running and of the flight of the falcon (Apollo's bird, cf. 15.526) which describe the movement and speed of this ship (*Od.* 13.81 ff.) are shamanic in association.

114. Stanford on *Od.* 8.556.

115. *Od.* 8.555 ff.

116. πολύφραστα, line 4; Guthrie's translation p. 7.

117. *Od.* 10.138.

118. *Od.* 12.3-4.

119. *Od.* 10.490 ff.

120. *Od.* 12.37 ff.; Hesiod works with the same tradition when he represents Circe as travelling on the Sun's chariot to the west (schol. Apoll. Rhod., *Arg.* 3.311 φησὶ δὲ 'Απολλώνιος 'Ησιόδῳ ἑπόμενος ἐπὶ τοῦ ἅρματος τοῦ 'Ηλίου εἰς τὴν κατὰ Τυρρηνίαν κειμένην νῆσον τὴν Κίρκην ἐλθεῖν (frag. 390 Merkelbach and West).

121. *Od.* 12.41 ff.

122. *Od.* 12.186 ff.

123. *Il.* 2.485-6.

124. *Od.* 17.517 ff.

125. R. B. Onians, *Origins of European Thought* (Cambridge, 1951), p. 368.

126. Ernst Buschor, *Die Musen des Jenseits* (München, 1944) *passim*.

127. E.g. Soph., frg. 777 (Nauck), Plato *Crat.* 403 D; Eurip., frg. 911 (Nauck), Plato, *repl.* 617 B.

128. Professor T. B. L. Webster has strongly urged this point with me more than once.

129. Webster, chapter 6. Kirk, chapter 6.

130. Dodds, op. cit., p. 142, p. 164, n. 47; Meuli, op. cit., pp. 1 ff.

131. Dodds, op. cit., p. 140; cf. Butterworth, op. cit., p. 153; cf. also Stuart Piggott, op. cit. *passim*.

132. Butterworth, op. cit., pp. 154 ff.

133. Walter Burkert, Γόης 'Zum griechischen "Schamanismus"', *Rheinisches Museum* 105, 1962, p. 47. For the possibility of very ancient Hittite influence or origin cf. the following: Webster, p. 123, 'his (Odysseus') wanderings are adapted from the Gilgamesh epic and in these wanderings he reaches

Phaeacia, which is a Mycenaean fairyland'. Eliade, pp. 78 and 313, n. 69: references to the Gilgamesh epic in shamanic context; Stuart Piggott, 'Heads and Hoofs', *Antiquity* 36, 1962, p. 115: possibility of shamanic features in Hittite burials.

## NOTES ON CHAPTER III

## GUEST - FRIENDSHIP

1. M. I. Finley, pp. 109 ff.
2. Herodotus 1.69.3.
3. Finley, p. 111.
4. Finley, p. 112.
5. *Od.* 17.415 ff.
6. Cf. Stanford, s.v. 'etiquette'.
7. *Od.* 1.119-20, 3.34 ff.; 1.310, 4.48 ff, 19.317 ff.
8. *Od.* 1.130 ff., 3.37 ff., 4.51 ff., 6.248 ff., 7.172 ff., 10.316, 14.45 ff.
9. *Od.* 1.123-4, 3.69-70, 4.60-2, 14.46-7.
10. *Od.* 1.311, 13.10 ff., 15.113 ff., 123 ff.
11. *Od.* 9.369-70, 20.296.
12. *Od.* 7.190 ff., 10.18 ff.
13. Cf. chapter VIII. pp. 72 ff.
14. *Od.* 3.1 ff., 4.1 ff., 6.186 ff.; cf. Walter Arend, *Die typischen Szenen bei Homer,* Problemata 7, Berlin, 1933, chapter 2, esp. pp. 40-44.
15. *Od.* 7.199 ff.
16. *Od.* 7.238.
17. *Od.* 8.28.
18. The interpretation of this song is difficult, because nothing but what is relevant to the context is mentioned, so that the whole is highly elliptic. It must be understood in relation to the other two songs.
19. *Od.* 8.81-2
20. Walter Marg, 'Das erste Lied des Demodokos', *Navicula Chiloniensis* to Felix Jacoby (Leiden, 1956) pp. 16-29, especially p. 23. While this paper is full of interest, its argumentation seems impossible to me, because it proceeds as if the poet of the *Odyssey* was working with a definitive written text of the *Iliad* for comparison.
21. Cf. chapter IX, pp. 80 ff.
22. *Il.* 9.312-3.

23. This is precisely what the scholiast proposes, and also Eustathius (cf. Merry and Riddell, ad loc.). The fact that we have no other evidence for this is unfortunate, but proves nothing. If we take the idea of epic as 'oral' poetry seriously, we must assume hundreds of stories and versions of stories about the Fall of Troy; and it makes a perfectly good story if we, with the scholiast, assume that after the death of Hector a dispute arose at a festive meal between Odysseus and Achilles, in which each one spoke out of his traditional character and powers, and then acted accordingly. Achilles fought, and died; Odysseus used guile, and conquered Troy. The references to the *Syndeipnoi* of Sophocles quoted by Merry and Riddell on *Od.* 8.75 and by Marg (op. cit., pp. 18-19, though critically) show that Sophocles worked with a tradition of a quarrel between Odysseus and Achilles. A corresponding tradition appears in the Sophoclean Philoctetes, where Odysseus and Neoptolemus, true son of Achilles, go together to fetch Philoctetes and his bow, but find that at the crucial moment Neoptolemus cannot but speak and act truthfully so that he betrays Odysseus' guile. Such tension, or even a mighty quarrel, does not necessarily permanently damage the friendship between heroes. For the character of Neoptolemus cf. *Philoct.* 90-1. ἀλλ' εἴμ' ἑτοῖμος πρὸς βίαν τὸν ἄνδρ' ἄγειν καὶ μὴ δόλοισιν, cf. 1282 ff.

24. *Od.* 8.329-332.
25. *Od.* 11.115-7; cf. Howard W. Charles, *The Art of the Odyssey* (Spectrum Book, 1967), p. 55.
26. *Od.* 8.550 ff.
27. *Od.* 15.193 ff.
28. *Od.* 4.589 ff.
29. *Od.* 15.104 ff.
30. *Od.* 8.392-3.
31. *Od.* 13.13 ff.
32. Cf. chapter VIII, pp. 72 ff.

NOTES ON CHAPTER IV

# TESTING

1. Cf. chapter I, *passim.*
2. *Od.* 21.188 ff.
3. Cf. *Od.* 19.390 ff.
4. *Od.* 24.235 ff.
5. *Od.* 4.117 ff.

6. *Od.* 23.85 ff.
7. *Od.* 14.459 ff.
8. *Od.* 15.304 ff.
9. Cf. chapter IX, pp. 86 ff. and chapter XI, p. 116.
10. *Od.* 19.65 ff.; cf. chapter IX, p. 86.
11. Cf. chapter IX, pp. 87 ff. and chapter XI, pp. 116-7.
12. *Od.* 24.329 ff.
13. Cf. above Phase 1.
14. *Od.* 23.174 ff., 181 ff.
15. *Od.* 19.215 ff.
16. *Od.* 21.243 ff.
17. *Od.* 24.361 ff., esp. 489 ff.; 23.355 ff.
18. Cf. note 9 above.
19. Peter G. Katzung, *Die Diapeira in der Iliashandlung* (Frankfurt dissertation, 1960), pp. 49-50.
20. *Il.* 2.73.
21. Cf. Theognis, 125-8; cf. H. Kleinknecht, 'Platonisches im Homer', *Gymnasium* 65, 1958, p. 69 who connects the dialogue between Athene and Odysseus in 13.221 ff. with the Socratic ἔλεγχος.

## NOTES ON CHAPTER V

## OMENS

1. *Od.* 2.157 ff.
2. *Od.* 15.531 ff.
3. *Od.* 15.172 ff.
4. *Od.* 2.158-9.
5. *Od.* 2.181-2.
6. φήμη, κληδών; cf. Amory, 'The Reunion of Odysseus and Penelope' in *Essays on the Odyssey*, p. 109, 110.
7. *Od.* 2.153 δρυψαμένω δ' ὀνύχεσσι παρειὰς ἀμφί τε δειράς means 'having torn their cheeks and their necks round about with their talons', not, as Merry and Riddell have it: 'having torn each other's cheeks and throats all about'. δρύπτεσθαι with παρειάν means 'to tear one's cheek in mourning' (cf. Liddell and Scott; cf. also ἀμφιδρυφής *Il.* 2.700 and ἀμφίδρυφος *Il.* 11.393). There is no point in mutual aggressiveness of the birds that symbolize Odysseus and Telemachus; rather they mourn about the situation in Ithaca.
8. *Od.* 2.162-3.
9. *Od.* 2.166-7.
10. *Od.* 15.160 ff.

11. *Od*. 19.535 ff.
12. *Od*. 20.242-3.
13. *Od*. 2.143 ff.
14. *Od*. 15.160 ff.
15. *Od*. 19.136.
16. *Od*. 19.512 ff.
17. *Od*. 20.241.
18. *Od*. 15.531 ff. and 17.152 ff.; cf. Page, pp. 84 ff.; Kirk, pp. 240-1.
19. *Od*. 15.521-2; cf. chapter III, p. 39.
20. *Od*. 15.523-4.
21. *Od*. 15.531-2.
22. Cf. Page, p. 85.
23. *Od*. 17.152 ff.
24. *Od*. 17.41 and 104 ff.; cf. chapter VI, pp. 61-2.
25. *Od*. 17.142 ff.
26. *Od*. 17.157 ff. The phrase ἥμενος ἢ ἕρπων goes with the following participle. ἥμενος implies idleness or inactivity. In 2.239 ff. Mentor upbraids the people of Ithaca for sitting in silence instead of preventing the Suitors from their evil-doing. In 10.374 ff. Odysseus just sits, and will not eat of the food that Circe puts before him, because his companions are still swine. In 16.145 Laertes no longer eats, nor drinks nor oversees the work, but just sits wailing. In each case, sitting is contrasted with action. The action in our passage is ἕρπων. This word denotes the movement proper to living beings, 18.131; in 12.395 it denotes the movement of the hides of the sungod's cattle which have been slaughtered. ἕρπω here has overtones of the uncanny, the ill-boding. This emotive shade may be, but does not have to be part of its meaning.
27. *Od*. 15.177-8.
28. *Od*. 15.156-7.
29. *Od*. 17.182 ff.
30. *Od*. 2.146 ff.
31. Cf. note 7 above.
32. *Od*. 15.160 ff.
33. *Od*. 15.525 ff.
34. *Od*. 19.535 ff.
35. *Od*. 20.241 ff.
36. Cf. also A. J. Podlecki, 'Omens in the *Odyssey*', *Greece and Rome*, 1967, vol. 14, pp. 12-23.
37. *Od*. 2.35; 18.117 and 20.100 ff.; 17.541.
38. *Od*. 20.103; 21.413; 24.539.
39. *Od*. 1.386; with this and the previous note cf. Amory, op. cit., p. 116 and p. 134, notes 48 and 49.

NOTES ON CHAPTER VI

## THEOCLYMENUS

1.  *Od*. 11.291.
2.  *Od*. 15.222 ff.
3.  Cf. H. and A. Thornton, *Time and Style* (Dunedin and London, 1962), chapter 1, *passim*.
4.  *Od*. 15.228, 238.
5.  Kirk, p. 242 concludes 'that Theoclymenus cannot have been conceived by the main poet especially for his part in the monumental *Odyssey;* he is an intrusive element, though when and why the intrusion was made we cannot tell'. I hope that the reasons for introducing Theoclymenus into the *Odyssey* will become plain presently. Hesiod was believed to have composed a *Melampodeia* of which a few fragments are in fact extant.
6.  Cf. Stanford on *Od*. 15.225; for the piecemeal, supplementary narrative cf. chapter I, p. 13.
7.  *Od*. 15.224 and 263-4; cf. Page, p. 84.
8.  *Od*. 15.525 ff.; cf. chapter V, p. 54.
9.  *Od*. 17.36 ff. Cf. Page's objections, pp. 85 and 87. The bath and the clean clothes have nothing to do with meeting a stranger. They are an act of purification prior to prayer and sacrifices. Cf. 4.750-9 where the prayer is not followed by meeting anybody.
10. *Od*. 16.303.
11. The apparent rudeness of Telemachus to his mother is therefore prompted by real concern for her. This seems not to be understood by Page, pp. 87-8, Kirk, p. 241 and A. B. Lord, *The Singer of Tales* (Harvard Univ. Press, 1960), pp. 171 ff., who says however that 'it is more likely that Telemachus' story had to be saved until Theoclymenus was present', p. 173. Lord misinterprets 17.104-6. He says: 'She (Penelope) asks him for the report stating that he had not dared to give it before because of the Suitors—yet the Suitors were not present at the time of his return' (p. 171). The lines surely mean: 'You could not bring yourself to tell me clearly about your father's return, if you heard of it anywhere, before the arrogant Suitors arrived in the house here' (for the translation of ἔτλης cf. Cunliffe (*s.v.* τλάω 7d). The first meeting between Penelope and Telemachus takes place soon after dawn when the Suitors have not yet arrived. Penelope had hoped for a private talk with Telemachus, without the restraints of the Suitors' presence.
12. *Od*. 20.351 ff.

13. Both Page p. 86 and Kirk p. 242 find the faculty of 'second sight' here displayed by Theoclymenus alien to the Homeric epic. It is certainly unique, but it is fitting.

## NOTES ON CHAPTER VII

## THE SUITORS

1. *Od*. 1.289-96.
2. Page imagines Telemachus as giving the following reply to the goddess (p. 56): 'I could understand and appreciate a command to kill the Suitors *before* the marriage of Penelope: but what on earth would be the point of delaying that action until after one of them has married her? Apart from that, do you not see that after the marriage there would be no Suitors left in my palace?' Page assumes here that the Suitors would leave the palace of Odysseus, once one of them had married Penelope. Cf. Kirk pp. 229-30.
3. *Od*. 2.87 ff.
4. Cf. chapter V, pp. 52-3.
5. *Od*. 18.288-9; 2.127-8.
6. *Od*. 20.334 ff.
7. *Od*. 19.533-4; cf. also 21.102-5.
8. *Od*. 16.361-2.
9. *Od*. 1.384-7, 400 ff.
10. *Od*. 2.242 ff.
11. *Od*. 21.250 ff.
12. *Od*. 18.245 ff.
13. *Od*. 22.48 ff.
14. *Od*. 1.250-1; 16.127-8.
15. *Od*. 2.55 ff., 142; 4.318 ff.; 14.81 ff.
16. *Od*. 14.99 ff.
17. *Od*. 1.250-1.
18. *Od*. 2.331 ff.
19. *Od*. 4.669 ff.; 4.770-1.
20. *Od*. 16.431-2.
21. *Od*. 18.275 ff.
22. *Od*. 21.68 ff.
23. *Od*. 18.144; 24.459.
24. *Cf*. Finley, pp. 91 ff.
25. Cf. chapter I, pp. 2-3, concerning the character of the Suitors.

## TELEMACHUS

1. Cf. W. J. Woodhouse, *The Composition of Homer's Odyssey* (Oxford, 1930), pp. 212-4; H. D. F. Kitto, *Poiesis* (Univ. of California Press, 1966) pp. 135-6.
2. *Od*. 1.321.
3. *Od*. 1.397-8. The 'supreme' king is only the 'first among equals' (Finley, pp. 114 ff.); but the other nobles who do not hold this supreme power are also called 'kings'.
4. *Od*. 1.320 ff., 420.
5. Cf. Friedrich Klingner, *Über die vier ersten Bücher der Odyssee* (Berichte über die Verh. d. Sächs. Akademie d. Wissenschaften z. Leipzig, Phil-hist. Klasse, vol. 96 Heft 1, 1944, pp. 18 ff.); Kitto, op. cit., pp. 136 ff.
6. *Od*. 4.638-40.
7. Cf. chapter IX, p. 78.
8. *Od*. 2.316.
9. *Od*. 2.409.
10. *Od*. 18.175-6.
11. *Od*. 18.269. Cf. chapter X, p. 98.
12. *Od*. 21.128-9.
13. *Od*. 24.515.
14. *Od*. 1.323, 420; 2.262 ff.
15. *Od*. 3.227-8.
16. *Od*. 3.231.
17. *Od*. 16.196-8.
18. *Od*. 16.211-12.
19. *Od*. 16.263-5.
20. Cf. Monro and Stanford ad loc.: have they overdone this?
21. *Od*. 16.320.
22. *Od*. 20.98 ff.; 21.415.
23. *Od*. 19.40.
24. Cf. chapter III.
25. *Od*. 1.119 ff.
26. *Od*. 1.310-11.
27. *Od*. 15.69 ff.
28. *Od*. 15.222 ff.
29. *Od*. 15.509 ff.
30. Cf. chapter III, p. 39.
31. *Od*. 15.533-4. Cf. chapter V, pp. 54-5.
32. *Od*. 16.69 ff.
33. *Od*. 16.99 ff.
34. *Od*. 16.274 ff.
35. *Od*. 17.345 ff.

36. *Od*. 18.34: this is the only time that he is called ἱερὸν μένος 'Αντινόοιο.
37. *Od*. 18.60: Telemachus is called ἱερὴ ἲς Τηλεμάχοιο as if to balance ἱερὸν μένος 'Αντινόοιο.
38. *Od*. 18.215 ff.
39. *Od*. 18.405. Telemachus is again called ἱερὴ ἲς Τηλεμάχοιο.
40. *Od*. 18.64.
41. *Od*. 20.257 ff.
42. *Od*. 20.317-9; 16.107-9.
43. Cf. above note 30.
44. *Od*. 21.281 ff.
45. *Od*. 21.312-3. Page, p. 128 and Kirk, p. 247 believe that Penelope here speaks out of her collusion with Odysseus. I shall try to show that this assumption is unwarranted; cf. chapter X, p. 101 and note 55.
46. *Od*. 21.353.
47. *Od*. 1.369.
48. *Od*. 24.505 ff.; cf. chapter XI, p. 118.


NOTES ON CHAPTER IX

ODYSSEUS

1. Werner Jäger, *Paideia*, vol. I, pp. 5-6.
2. *Od*. 18.228-9.
3. *Od*. 2.117 ff., cf. chapter X, p. 95. Cf. on this and the following Herwig Maehler, 'Die Auffassung des Dichterberufs im frühen Griechentum bis zur Zeit Pindars', *Hypomnemata* 3, 1963, Göttingen, p. 23. Cf. W. B. Stanford, *The Ulysses Theme* (Oxford, 1954), pp. 25.42.
4. *Od*. 13.298-9.
5. *Od*. 13.297-8.
6. Cf. H. W. Clarke, *The Art of the Odyssey*, Spectrum Book, 1967, pp. 76-7.
7. *Od*. 1.260 ff.
8. *Od*. 8.215 ff.
9. *Od*. 11.606-8.
10. *Od*. 19.572 ff.
11. The differences between the actual removal of arms in Book 19 and the planning for it in Book 16.281 ff. remain difficult. The solution probably lies in the direction indicated by Karl Büchner, 'Die Waffenbergung in der Odyssee', *Hermes* 67, 1932, pp. 438-45.
12. Cf. *Od*. 8.224 ff.

13. *Od*. 21.411.
14. *Od*. 22.109 ff.
15. *Od*. 24.167 ff.
16. *Od*. 1.66, 3.122, 9.19-20.
17. *Od*. 9.502 ff.
18. *Od*. 12.210 ff.; in all probability the contrast drawn between Achilles and Odysseus rests on the contrast between physical force and power of intelligence, cf. chapter III, pp. 43-4.
19. *Od*. 4.267 ff.; cf. H. Fränkel's description of the character of Odysseus where this aspect is represented as central (*Dichtung und Philosophie des frühen Griechentums*, New York, 1951, pp. 123-4).
20. *Od*. 9.299 ff.
21. *Od*. 20.9 ff.; cf. Stanford ad loc.
22. *Od*. 20.23; cf. Stanford ad loc. on ἐν πείσῃ, and Monro who quotes a scholion: ἐν δεσμοῖς.
23. *Od*. 12.192 ff.
24. *Od*. 13.221 ff.
25. Cf. note 72 below.
26. *Od*. 13.332.
27. Proposed by Wackernagel and preferred by Stanford.
28. *Od*. 13.298; Stanford's objection that ἐπητής shows no trace of a digamma has no force when it is taken into account that the digamma is at times neglected in ἔπος, cf. P. Chantraine, *Grammaire Homérique* (Paris, 1948), vol. I, pp. 133-4.
29. Cf. *Lexikon des frühgriechischen Epos*, ed. Snell and Mette (Göttingen, 1955) *s.v.* ἀγχίθεος; reference to Ernst Risch, *Wortbildung der homerischen Sprache* (Berlin, 1937), par. 69.
30. This image of tight-togetherness, with no gaps or interstices, and its opposite of 'spreadoutness' or 'being relaxed' are characteristic of Homeric and later Greek notions about a self-possessed and intelligent person and a stupid, impulse-driven person; cf. chapter X, p. 97; cf. H. Kleinknecht, 'Platonisches im Homer', *Gymnasium* 65, 1958 (p. 69) who gives 'Geistesgegenwart' for ἀγχίνοος.
31. Cunliffe, *s.v.* ἐχέφρων.
32. *Od*. 8.320.
33. *Od*. 13.333 ff.
34. *Od*. 13.335; δαήμεναι οὐδὲ πυθέσθαι cannot refer to Odysseus asking someone outside the family eager questions about his family, as Stanford takes it, for the specifically stated time-sequence would be senseless. 'It is *not yet* pleasing to you to learn and find out.' Since a direct test of a person is the most reliable evidence anyone can have about a person,

much more reliable than asking other people about him, this sentence is absurd, if 'to learn and find out' can only refer to inquiry from someone else. But in Book 23.262 Penelope uses the two verbs when she wants Odysseus to tell her about the task and the travel that lies still ahead of him about which he heard from Tiresias in the Underworld. She asks therefore about the past and also about the future. Similarly here, Odysseus does not yet want to ask Penelope about her past experiences, not until he has tested her. Husband and wife exchange their tales after the recognition scene (23.300 ff.).

35. Cf. Conclusion, p. 123.
36. *Od*. 13.333 ff.
37. *Od*. 18.427-8.
38. *Od*. 19.1 ff.
39. *Od*. 19.44-6; Penelope's purpose in asking the beggar questions has been made plain earlier 17.554 ff.; cf. 19.93 ff.
40. Testing Type I, Phase 2, cf. chapter IV, p. 49.
41. *Od*. 9.494.
42. Cf. *Il*. 17.658.
43. *Il*. 1.32.
44. Cf. also *Il*. 24.560 ff. and ἐρέθω *Il*. 3.414 ff.
45. *Od*. 20.373-4.
46. Cf. also *Od*. 17.394 ff.
47. *Il*. 4.5.
48. *Il*. 5.419 ff.
49. *Od*. 16.304 ff.
50. *Od*. 18.307 ff.
51. *Od*. 19.45.
52. Cf. pp. 81-2 above.
53. *Od*. 22.457 ff.
54. *Od*. 19.83.
55. *Od*. 19.107; cf. Stanford ad loc.
56. *Od*. 2.230 ff.; 5.8 ff.
57. To this archaic outlook 'Dike, Order', as Professor H. D. F. Kitto says (*Poiesis*, Univ. of California Press, 1966, p. 134) 'is indivisible; the moral, physical and (here) economic worlds are one.'
58. *Od*. 19.120; Penelope has heard this line before. It was spoken reproachfully to her by her maid Eurynome although the maid could hardly understand Penelope's very mixed feelings at Telemachus' growing-up, 18.174.
59. *Od*. 19.124 ff.
60. Cf. the just and the unjust cities in Hesiod's *Erga* 225 ff. where the outlook is the same.
61. Cf. chapter X, p. 98.

62. There is no need to suppose that Penelope thinks or vaguely apprehends that the beggar is Odysseus.

63. *Od.* 19.209 ff.

64. On horn as a substance cf. Anne Amory, 'The Gates of Horn and Ivory', *Yale Classical Studies*, vol. 20, 1966, pp. 43 ff.

65. Stanford op. cit., p. 7 speaks of 'the inherent ethical ambiguity of his (*scil.* Odysseus') distinctive characteristic among the Homeric heroes—which is intelligence. Intelligence, as Homer indicates, is a neutral quality. It may take the form of low and selfish cunning or of exalted, altruistic wisdom.' I do not think that to call intelligence in Homer 'neutral' makes the matter sufficiently clear; and the ideas of 'selfishness' and 'altruism' are Christian, not Homeric. The same applies to *dolos* (cf. Stanford, op. cit., p. 249, n. 17) as to intelligence. Both intelligence and its main manifestation 'guile' are highly prized when they work for yourself, are dangerous when they threaten you and yours, and are evil when they are used unjustly; but usually they are highly prized. Further, the use of the word 'ethical' in relation to Homer is fraught with difficulty because, as E. R. Dodds, *The Greeks and the Irrational* (Univ. of California Press, 1951) has pointed out, Homeric society is a 'shame-culture', while ethics in our modern sense belongs to a 'guilt-culture'. Homeric 'ethics' is primarily determined by honour and glory, by the limited social unit of the οἶκος and by Zeus as the upholder of justice.

66. *Od.* 6.180 ff.; 6.184-5 . . . πολλ' ἄλγεα δυσμενέεσσι, χάρματα δ' εὐμενέτῃσι. μάλιστα δέ τ' ἔκλυον αὐτοί, Standford ad loc.: ' " . . a great grief to their foes and a joy to their friends; but they know it best themselves" (Murray). This use of κλύω is unparalleled, but it seems to be the meaning required by the context, cp. μάλιστα δὲ καὐτὸς ἀνέγνω in *Il.* 13.734 . . . ' As Stanford says, κλύω does not mean 'I know'. What one ought to expect here is the idea that this man and this woman gain fame through their harmonious life, while their enemies gain grief and their friends joy; just as in *Il.* 4.179 (= 207) Agamemnon says about wounded Menelaus: 'whom someone struck with an arrow, skilled in archery, one of the Trojans or the Lycians, to him fame, but to us grief.' I suggest that κλύω is here used as the passive for εἰπεῖν (cf. *Od.* 19.334), just as κλύω in tragedy and ἀκούω in post-Homeric Greek generally are used for the passive of λέγω (cf. Liddell and Scott). The sentence means then that people talk a great deal about them, whether with delight or fear: it makes that couple famous. Cf. also the meaning

of thc name 'Odysseus' as 'he who causes pain' (G. E. Dimock, 'The Name of Odysseus' in *Essays on the Odyssey*, p. 55).
67. Cf. the notion of justice attributed to Homer and the other poets in Plato, *repl*. 1.334 b.
68. Cf. Finley, see index under 'household'.
69. Cf. above p. 80.
70. *Od*. 9.406.
71. *Od*. 1.296.
72. *Od*. 5.356 ff.; 10.380; cf. also Eurylochus 10.232, 258.
73. Cf. chapter I, esp. note 8.
74. *Od*. 11.439; 24.200 ff.; it is striking that δολόμητις, 'guile-minded' is used once of Clytemnestra and five times of Aegisthus and of no one else. Aegisthus is of course the prototype of the evildoer in the *Odyssey* (cf. chapter I, p. 2); there is a tendency here towards the later negative connotation of δόλος.
75. *Od*. 11.441 ff.
76. *Od*. 13.383 ff.
77. *Od*. 4.267 ff., cf. above pp. 80-1; 20.6 ff., cf. above pp. 81-2.
78. Cf. chapter X, pp. 104-5.
79. *Od*. 19.212.
80. *Od*. 13.332.

## NOTES ON CHAPTER X

### PENELOPE

1. *Od*. 2.120 ff.; cf. 11.235 ff., 266 ff.
2. Cf. Stanford on *Od*. 18.195-6; also Nestor's daughter Pero 11.287.
3. *Od*. 21.6; 6.128.
4. *Od*. 18.195; 6.230, 23.157.
5. *Od*. 1.334-5; 18.210-1.
6. *Od*. 18.212-3.
7. *Od*. 18.160; cf. chapter IX, p. 83 and note 30.
8. Cf. below p. 98 and chapter IX, p. 90 on the importance of treasure.
9. *Od*. 24.193 ff.; cf. chapter I, p. 10.
10. Cf. R. B. Onians, *Origins of European Thought* (Cambridge, 1951), pp. 13-5.
11. Cf. above p. 93; *Od*. 2.88 and 117-8.
12. *Od*. 2.93.

13. Kirk assumes p. 244 that 'Penelope had been found out some considerable time before, and since then had been employing other delaying tactics.' (cf. also Page, pp. 120-1 and W. J. Woodhouse, *The Composition of Homer's Odyssey* (Oxford, 1930), p. 70). But there is no need to assume that the guile of the web preceded the guile of the deceptive messages to each Suitor. The line of transition between the two guiles is (93): ἡ δὲ δόλον τόνδ' ἄλλον ἐνὶ φρεσὶ μερμήριξε. If this is translated as 'And she has thought out in her heart the following trick in addition', the sending of messages and the weaving of the web can be simultaneous (for ἄλλος as 'additional' or 'in addition' cf. Cunliffe *s.v.* II 1a). The similar time span of the weaving (just over three years 2.106-7; 19.151-2) and of the sending of messages (almost three years 2.89) is neither 'deceptive' nor suggests 'a mechanical and localized expansion' (Kirk, p. 245), but it indicates the contemporaneity of the two actions. This is what one must expect in view of Athene's words to Odysseus that 'the Suitors have been lording it in his house for three years' 13.377. All this means that the finishing of the web must be thought of as quite recent in Book 2.

14. *Od.* 4.678.

15. *Od.* 4.739.

16. *Od.* 13.303, 386.

17. *Od.* 5.356.

18. *Od.* 9.422.

19. *Il.* 6.187; 3.212.

20. *Od.* 2.89 ff.; 19.138 ff.; 24.128 ff.

21. While the ancient allegorists went too far in taking the web to be a 'web of dialectic which with its subtle and prolonged arguments delayed the Suitors' (Stanford on *Od.* 2.94), the web is more than a mere actual piece of weaving: it is also a work of cunning and intelligence, and as such suggestive of Penelope's purpose in weaving it.

22. *Od.* 2.117-8.

23. *Od.* 15.107-8.

24. *Od.* 13.189 ff., cf. Stanford ad loc. on ὄφρα; the purpose of the mist is also to hide Odysseus and so prevent any chance recognition, cf. 7.15 ff. and 39 ff.

25. *Od.* 13.308-9.

26. *Od.* 16.301-3.

27. *Od.* 21.188 ff.

28. It has been variously suggested that Penelope more or less consciously recognizes Odysseus in the course of Book 19 (Anne Amory, 'The Reunion of Odysseus and Penelope' in *Essays on the Odyssey*, pp. 105 ff.; W. B. Stanford, *The*

*Ulysses Theme* (Oxford, 1954), p. 55, and further references p. 253, n. 25). In view of the passages quoted above, particularly Athene's intention in 13.190 ff., it seems impossible to me to assume that Homer intended this. Cf. Fr. Eichhorn, *Homer's Odyssee, Ein Führer durch die Dichtung* (Göttingen, 1965), p. 23, who also quotes U. v. Wilamowitz, *Die Heimkehr des Odysseus* (1927), p. 46.

29. *Od*. 18.160; cf. below n. 32 and chapter IX, n. 30.
30. Cf. Page, p. 124, who argues convincingly that this is Athene's purpose, and not Penelope's.
31. *Od*. 18.175-6.
32. *Od*. 18.212-3; cf. above n. 29.
33. *Od*. 1.360 ff.; 4.817-8.
34. *Od*. 18.217.
35. *Od*. 18.269-70.
36. *Od*. 18.282-3.
37. Cf. *Od*. 2.93 and 13.381.
38. *Od*. 17.553 ff., cf. on all this Page, p. 124, whose arguments do not seem to me to be convincing. Odysseus rejoices at her cleverness and loyalty to him in striving to increase the wealth of his house.
39. Cf. chapter IX, pp. 87 ff.
40. *Od*. 19.124-9 = 18.251-6; cf. chapter IX, pp. 87-88.
41. *Od*. 19.134 ff.
42. *Od*. 19.157 ff.
43. *Od*. 19.215 ff.; Type 2 Testing; cf. chapter IV, p. 50.
44. *Od*. 19.249 ff. These are the fifth and sixth phases of Penelope's countertesting.
45. *Od*. 19.253-4.
46. *Od*. 19.257-8.
47. *Od*. 19.299.
48. Cf. chapter IX, p. 90 and Finley, see index, s.v. 'treasure'.
49. Cf. chapter IV, p. 49.
50. *Od*. 17.44 and 101 ff.
51. *Od*. 17.507 ff.
52. *Od*. 18.202 ff.
53. *Od*. 19.312 ff.
54. *Od*. 19.134.
55. *Od*. 19.317 ff.; the following point raised by Page, p. 128 and Kirk, p. 247, connects with this: Kirk says: 'Lastly, when the Suitors have failed to string the bow Penelope herself insists at surprising length that it should be given to the stranger to try—a poorly motivated insistence if she really thought him a humble stranger' (21.312 ff.). Kirk means that this insistence is only intelligible if Penelope knows that the beggar is Odysseus. Her insistence is however

perfectly plausible in view of her desire to offer all possible hospitality to her husband's old guest-friend.

56. *Od*. 19.347.

57. *Od*. 19.373-4. This is a perfectly good reason; and it is unnecessary as Page, p. 126, and Kirk, p. 246, do, to assume another reason, such as that Odysseus wanted to be recognized by Eurycleia.

58. There is no good reason for complicating matters here: Odysseus had forgotten about his scar—quite simply.

59. Cf. H. and A. Thornton, *Time and Style* (Dunedin and London, 1962), Chapter 1, *passim*.

60. *Od*. 19.468.

61. *Od*. 19.479; cf. Athene's intention 13.192-3, and p. 96.

62. *Od*. 19.159-61.

63. *Od*. 19.530 ff.

64. *Od*. 1.166 ff.

65. *Od*. 14.68.

66. *Od*. 14.122 ff.

67. *Od*. 14.149 ff.

68. *Od*. 14.167.

69. *Od*. 14.363 ff.

70. *Od*. 14.379.

71. *Od*. 14.391-2.

72. *Od*. 21.217 ff.

73. Cf. Amory, op. cit., p. 105, and p. 132, n. 19.

74. *Od*. 23.5 ff. For this scene between Penelope and Eurycleia cf. W. Schadewaldt, 'Neue Kriterien zur Odyssee-Analyse' (Sitzs. Heidelb. Akad. d. Wiss., 1959, 2te Aufl., 1966), pp. 13-5.

75. *Od*. 23.85 ff.; cf. chapter IV, p. 49.

76. *Od*. 23.117-163; Page, p. 114 and Schadewaldt, op. cit., pp. 12 ff. consider this to be an interpolation. It has however its own clear function. Schadewaldt also rejects lines 164-72 so that Penelope's words in 174 ff. become her answer to Odysseus' words in 113-6. This does violence to the poetic construction. For Odysseus' words in 113-6 are not directed to Penelope. Rather: before the interlude both Odysseus and Penelope speak to Telemachus and so indirectly to each other. After the interlude, Odysseus speaks directly to Penelope, taunting her, and she replies.

77. *Od*. 23.115-6. It must be remembered that Odysseus is still in beggar's rags and covered with gore from the battle.

78. Cf. W. B. Stanford, *The Ulysses Theme* (Oxford, 1954), p. 57.

79. *Od*. 23.215 ff.

80. *Od*. 23.230.

81. Cf. chapter IX, p. 83.
82. Cf. Stanford, op. cit., p. 58.
83. Kirk says, p. 246, that 'Penelope's announcement of the trial of the bow, at the end of that conversation, is utterly illogical' and that she does so 'apparently without special reason'; Page says, p. 126, that 'Penelope's sudden announcement of her surrender to the Suitors runs absolutely counter to all that has preceded, unless she has recognized Odysseus in the meantime.' If of course one removes one of the great carrying-posts of a building, as Woodhouse, op. cit., does when he assumes, pp. 86 f., that Odysseus' parting words are an invention of Penelope's, one cannot be surprised if the building collapses; neither Page nor Kirk mentions Odysseus' parting words. Both make much of the rising sequence of omens and prophecies etc., but there are good reasons for Penelope's unbelief. Eichhorn, op. cit., p. 23, also believes that those parting words are invented by Penelope; he further assumes that the bow contest is also a trick of Penelope's to gain time, because she does not believe that any of the Suitors will be able to string the bow. This assumption is impossible because Penelope says explicitly that she can no longer find a 'way out', 19.157-8. Whether in fact Antinous or Eurymachus could have strung the bow, we are never told; and it is idle to speculate about it.
84. *Od*. 24.121 ff.
85. *Od*. 24.167-8; cf. Stanford ad loc.
86. Kirk, p. 245.
87. *Od*. 17.544.
88. Stanford ad loc.
89. Cf. chapter IX, pp. 81 ff.
90. *Od*. 1.197 ff.
91. *Od*. 1.14, 48 ff.
92. *Od*. 7.299 ff.
93. *Od*. 6.273 ff.
94. *Od*. 4.770-1.
95. Stanford, vol. II, p. lvi.
96. Finley, pp. 96 and 99.
97. Finley, p. 97; cf. also Kirk, pp. 141-2.
98. *Od*. 1.346 ff.
99. *Od*. 2.130 ff.
100. *Od*. 21.344 ff.
101. *Od*. 2.113-4.
102. *Od*. 15.16 7.
103. *Od*. 18.266-70.
104. *Od*. 19.525 ff.

105. *Od*. 2.225 ff.
106. *Od*. 2.229 ff.; cf. Finley, p. 101.
107. Cf. above pp. 100-101.
108. *Od*. 18.275 ff.
109. *Od*. 11.174 ff.
110. *Od*. 1.389 ff. and 400-404.
111. *Od*. 19.528-9.
112. *Od*. 16.392.
113. *Od*. 15.17-8.
114. *Od*. 16.76-7 and 20.335.
115. *Od*. 18.289 and 11.179.
116. W. Jaeger, *Paideia, The Ideals of Greek Culture* (Oxford, 1954), vol. 1, p. 6; cf. chapter IX, p. 78.
117. Cf. Jaeger, op. cit., p. 7; Finley, p. 131 f.; A. W. H. Adkins, *Merit and Responsibility* (Oxford, 1960), pp. 30 ff.; and esp. p. 40; cf. *Il*. 6.208.
118. *Od*. 4.626; 17.167; cf. Finley, loc. cit.
119. *Od*. 18.277.
120. *Od*. 21.106 ff.
121. *Od*. 2.115 ff.
122. *Od*. 2.206.
123. Cf. chapter IX, pp. 78-80.
124. *Od*. 15.519 ff.
125. Cf. chapter V. pp. 54-5.
126. Cf. chapter VII. pp. 64-5.
127. Finley, pp. 91 ff.
128. *Od*. 1.387.
129. *Od*. 21.128.
130. *Od*. 21.77 ff.
131. *Od*. 18.270.
132. *Od*. 16.385-6.

## NOTES ON CHAPTER XI

## LAERTES

1. *Od*. 1.189 ff.
2. *Od*. 2.227.
3. *Od*. 4.735 ff.
4. *Od*. 11.195-6.
5. *Od*. 11.202-3.
6. *Od*. 16.139 ff.
7. *Od*. 24.231.
8. Stanford on *Od*. 24.231, referring to Hayman.

9. *Od*. 24.238. The hesitation of a character whether or not to test a person before revealing his identity is part of the traditional theme of testing (cf. chapter IV, pp. 48-9), and can therefore not be used for any speculation about composition, as A. B. Lord does in *The Singer of Tales* (Harvard Univ. Press, 1960), p. 179.

10. *Il*. 4.5-6; 5.419.

11. *Il*. 4.23-4.

12. *Il*. 5.421.

13. Cf. Stanford, on *Od*. 24.240.

14. *Od*. 24.242.

15. Any immediate recognition for which Odysseus had hoped (217-8) is hereby excluded.

16. *Od*. 24.248.

17. *Od*. 24.257.

18. *Od*. 24.248.

19. *Od*. 24.289-90. The phrase εἴ ποτ' ἔην is by some taken as 'the natural expression of a sad heart recalling a former joy or happiness now so utterly lost as to seem to have been but a dream.' Stanford on 15.268 quotes this, and agrees with it. It seems to me a type of romantic sentimentality which is quite alien to Homer. Monro, on 15.268, takes it as an 'assurance', and compares also *Il*. 3.180 and 11.762. The line means then: 'Your guest-friend, an unhappy man, my son, as surely as he lived, an ill-fated man.' It is the emphatic affirmation that this guest-friend was Odysseus, his son, with the implication that he himself is Laertes, which is needed here.

20. Cf. Stanford on *Od*. 24.304 ff.

21. *Od*. 24.328-9.

22. *Od*. 24.351-2.

23. Page, p. 112, describes the scene as follows: 'He (*scil*. Odysseus) plays upon his father's emotions until the old man is almost insensible from sorrow: then suddenly he springs the truth upon him.' This is hardly the sequence of events. When Odysseus reveals himself, Laertes asks for a sign, because he does not fully believe him. He does not faint until he recognizes the signs and the truth with them.

24. Cf. chapter IV, pp. 48 ff.

25. Page, p. 112, can see no sense in it (cf. also Kirk, p. 250, who refers to Lord, p. 178). Lord, op. cit., pp. 177 ff. defends 'the recognition of the returned hero by his parent' as 'a well-established element in the general story of return'; but he is troubled by 'its position in the poem'. The difficulty for him is the fact that during his meeting with Laertes Odysseus is not disguised, even though he tells him a decep-

tive story. He therefore suggests that this scene was originally intended for an earlier place in the epic. I believe that Odysseus' disguise having grown very thin in the course of the tale (cf. Conclusion, p. 128 on the gradual thinning of Odysseus' disguise) consists by now in the change wrought by 20 years of hard living and, on the other hand, in the old man's attitude (κατέχων κεφαλήν) which expresses his withdrawn and grieving loneliness, and which shuts him off from everybody else.

26. *Od*. 24.375 ff.
27. *Od*. 24.515.
28. Finley, p. 84.
29. Cf. Finley, p. 116.
30. Cf. Webster, p. 239.
31. *Od*. 11.174 and 492 ff.
32. *Od*. 4.741; cf. also 14.171 ff. and 181-2.
33. *Od*. 24.508-9.

NOTES ON CONCLUSION

# THE STRUCTURE OF THE ODYSSEY

1. I here follow closely Otfrid Becker, 'Das Bild des Weges', *Hermes* Einzelschrift 4, 1937, pp. 36, 68-9; cf. also W. K. C. Guthrie, *A History of Greek Philosophy* (Cambridge, 1965) vol. 2, p. 12: 'The equation "road or journey = quest for knowledge = lay or narrative conveying the results of that quest" was not his (i.e. Parmenides') own, but already present in the shamanistic practices of which his poem contains distinct though far-off echoes'; Guthrie refers to Meuli, 'Scythica', *Hermes* 70 (1935) p. 172 who says: 'now, the journey of the shaman, his main activity, is so completely identical with his song that the expression denoting a 'journey" has become a very common formula for a "song" in shamanic poetry.' Meuli goes on to compare the Homeric use of the word οἴμη. The use of this word suggests a very ancient and pervasive tradition derived from shamanism.
2. *Od*. 8.72 ff.
3. *Od*. 8.492-3.
4. *Od*. 8.481; 22.347-8.
5. Cf. Introduction, p. xiv.
6. Fr. Eichhorn in his *Homers Odyssee. Ein Führer durch die Dichtung* (Göttingen, 1965) also divides up the *Odyssey* into six parts which coincide with four books in each case, except for his division between the third and the fourth part at

13.92 (cf. my note 15 below). I do not agree with Eichhorn's division of each of the six parts into three sub-groups; the grouping into the traditional four 'books' seems more adequate to me.

7. *Od*. 1.84 ff.
8. Cf. chapter VIII.
9. Cf. chapter I, pp. 1 ff.
10. Eichhorn, op. cit., pp. 33-5.
11. *Od*. 5.29 ff.
12. Cf. chapter II, pp. 16-19.
13. Cf. chapter II. pp. 32-3; cf. Charles H. Taylor, Jr., 'The Obstacles to Odysseus' Return', *Essays on the Odyssey*: I find pp. 87-93 (top) excellent. But the assumption of an opposition of Olympian and chthonic forces and the use of the idea of the 'unconscious' in an interpretation of things Homeric seem out of place to me.
14. *Od*. 13.404 ff.
15. Eichhorn, op. cit. pp. 63 ff. assumes that the third lap begins at 8.470, with the third song of Demodocus and ends with 13.92 with Odysseus fast asleep as he is being taken to Ithaca. But the three songs of Demodocus seem to me to be part and parcel of a closely knit composition and therefore inseparable (cf. chapter III, pp. 42 ff.); John L. Myres' division between 13.197 and 198 does not seem feasible either ('The Pattern of the *Odyssey*', *JHS* 72, 1952, p. 3).
16. *Od*. 17.231-2, 406 ff., 462 ff.
17. *Od*. 18.394 ff.
18. *Od*. 20.299 ff.; cf. A. Lesky, 'Der Forschungsbericht Homer', 4. Forts., 2. Teil. *Anzeiger* f.d. *Altertumswiss*. vol. 18, 1/2 Heft, 1965, col. 27.
19. Cf. chapter IX, pp. 86 ff.
20. Cf. chapter VI, pp. 61-2.
21. *Od*. 21.4.
22. Cf. chapter X, pp. 104 ff.
23. Cf. chapter XI.
24. Cf. Eichhorn, op. cit.: titles for the six parts.
25. Aristotle, *Poetics* 24. 1459 b 15.
26. Uvo Hölscher, 'Untersuchungen zur Form der Odyssee, Szenenwechsel und gleichzeitige Handlungen', *Hermes*, Einzelschrift 6 (1939), p. 67.
27. Hermann quoted by I. Bywater in his commentary (Oxford, 1909) on Aristotle's *Poetics* 1459 b 15.
28. Cf. chapter III, p. 41.
29. *Od*. 1.235, 242; for the rich and varied meaning of the word καλύπτω cf. R. B. Onians, *The Origins of European Thought* (Cambridge, 1951) pp. 420 ff.

30. *Od*. 4.556 ff.
31. Cf. chapter II, p. 17.
32. *Od*. 7.237 ff.
33. *Od*. 9.19 ff.
34. Cf. chapter II, p. 17.
35. *Od*. 8.562.
36. *Od*. 13.29 ff. and 93 ff.
37. *Od*. 8.563.
38. *Od*. 13.163.
39. *Od*. 13.152, 158, 183. It is not altogether clear whether the 'rock-ship' *is* the mighty mountain, or whether the mountain is something threatened over and above.
40. Cf. chapter IX, p. 82 for details on this scene.
41. Cf. chapter IV.
42. *Od*. 16.172 ff.; cf. Stanford on *Od*. 16.213, and W. J. Woodhouse, *The Composition of Homer's Odyssey* (Oxford, 1930), pp. 77-8.
43. *Od*. 16.455 ff.
44. *Od*. 19.381 ff., 391 ff.
45. Cf. Page, pp. 88 ff.; Kirk, p. 243.
46. *Od*. 18.67 ff.
47. *Od*. 23.115-6.

# INDEX

## GENERAL INDEX

(All numerals in bold indicate pages in the text; other numerals refer to chapters and notes)

## INDEX OF PASSAGES CITED

(Numerals in bold indicate pages in this book; numerals in brackets are the numbers of notes to which readers are referred from these pages)